THE WAY OF RESPONSE

THE WAY OF RESPONSE

RESPONSE

Martin Buber

SELECTIONS FROM HIS WRITINGS EDITED BY

N. N. GLATZER

SCHOCKEN BOOKS ◑ NEW YORK

Contents

PROLOGUE: RESPONSE

I GOD

II I AND THOU

III FAITH

VII COMMUNITY AND HISTORY

VIII ISRAEL: JEWISH EXISTENCE

EPILOGUE: RENEWAL

Preface

○

Martin Buber's writings, in the course of six decades, document manifold interests, issues, and concerns. But through all of them runs one major motif: the motif of response. Buber's man is a responding man. Response establishes him as a person. The attitude of dialogue creates the sphere of authentic existence. This is the realm between the one who calls and the one who answers, the one who summons and the one who responds, the one who commands and the one who fulfils.

Nietzsche's dictum that "in the end one experiences only oneself" is counterposed by Buber's view that it is the other through whom I become fully I: if with my whole being I enter into a relationship with him. Ivan Karamazov's outcry, "I accept God but I do not accept his world," is opposed by Buber's conception of the world as the path to God, and of God's word as directing man toward action in the world. Sartre's and Camus' absurd man and absurd universe are counteracted by Buber's tenet of an unceasing, meaningful dialogue between heaven and earth, I and Thou, call and response.

Against impersonal man moving aimlessly in an impersonal universe, namelessly (K in Kafka's writing) in an anonymous world from which God has withdrawn, Buber affirms the personality of man—and of God. Man, capable of love, "personalizes all that he loves" (Unamuno) and discovers the element of personality in the All. Spinoza, initiating modern thought, decided to remove this element from his view of God and man, and thereby to amend the teaching of classical Israel and Christianity. Buber, fully aware of the prevailing tendencies in modern science, psychology, and art, dared to reintroduce man's uniqueness—his personality —as a central issue in modern thought.

Buber's view that man's personality is determined by his ability to respond was born out of crises in his own life: the crisis of the young boy—son of divorced parents—told that the mother would never return to him; the crisis of the writer on the threshold of fame who failed to respond to a young man who (unknown to Buber, of course) contemplated suicide. Personal crises imparted an awareness of the crisis situation confronting man, communities, and nations: situations in which no set rule can be of help, problems that cannot be solved by application of some previously found solution. Here human response, and that alone, can be of any avail.

Since modern, Western, man incorporates the issues of the past in the range of his present concerns, Buber, in dealing with historical material, actually addresses himself to the preoccupation of contemporary thought and ultimately to one question: man's position in the world.

Though rooted in the heritage of classical Israel and in the initial period of his mature life speaking primarily to the Jewish community, Buber used tradition and the example of Judaism to buttress his understanding of man as man, of human individuality, predicament, and quest for meaning. In the last period of his life, the appeal to man in general became more and more articulate and urgent. What was nascent in the first period and sketchily announced (*I and Thou* is not a final testimony, only a sketch) attained fulfilment in the second, speaking with a mighty voice. Transcending the boundaries set by language, nationality, race, and specific religious commitment, he addressed himself not to some nebulous humanity, but to the human person everywhere.

Commonly, an anthology attempts to present a variety of moods, points of view, and styles of a given period, or a variety of themes and subject matter dealt with by an author. The present selection has a somewhat different purpose: it takes as its focus this single motif, the motif of response, that asserts itself in Buber's writings with ever-increasing power and persuasion. Expressed in a vast variety of forms, which Buber's linguistic discernment enabled him to give to this one thought, it is not circumscribed in any strict sense. Whatever seemed appropriate to elucidate it is included. Pertinent biographical references are given as part of the selection's over-all intent.

Buber is a master of the concise, epigrammatic statement, especially when the argument or discourse or address reaches the point when what matters most is about to be uttered. The selection attempts to do justice to this salient fact in Buber's writings. However, the interested reader is invited to pursue the full argument, the context of the central statement, by consulting the bibliographical guide, where the date, sources, and translation of each selection are recorded. With some exceptions, the individual titles are the editor's. The English renditions have been retained, with only minor changes.

Most of his interpreters view Buber's concern with the human condition and the way he pointed out for the man of today to follow—responsibility assumed out of an attitude of response—as his chief contribution to contemporary thought. The notion that what happens to man is but a summons to him, that his life is a series of dialogical situations—this teaching of Buber's may become increasingly important, or, at the very least, challenging, as we move on farther into an era of mass civilization, mass communication, and mass destiny, where individual man loses significance and individual life's meaning is called into question.

To whom does Buber speak? Naturally, to everyone who cares to listen. But, actually, to whom? Not to the philosopher as philosopher, not to the theologian as theologian, but to the human person in both and in everyone. Not to those who argue well and master the art of intellectual debate, but to those who in speech and answer are able to establish communion. To the simple: the farmer, the laborer, the searching student, the naïvely pious, the sincerely unbelieving. In dealing with the immense Hasidic literature, Buber disregarded its intricate theology and concentrated on the folk tales and legends where the heart speaks, where the unsophisticated but serious questioner is satisfied with the pointed but simple answer that faith can provide.

Yet, simplicity is a rare phenomenon, occupying a narrow field between the vast areas of ignorance and unconcern on the one hand, and specialized, conceptualized knowledge on the other. But Buber's writings reveal a profound trust in man's capacity to overcome the complexity created by his powers of observation, of forming theories, of knowledge in the Western sense, and to regain the simplicity that is related to knowledge in the Biblical sense, where it connotes love, an attitude of concern for the created world, and active participation in the perfection of this world.

But the emphasis on mutual personal relationship and on simplicity should not be apprehended as implying a narrowness of interest or outlook. Buber's humanist message must be viewed against the panoramic background of his learning in the fields of comparative religion, mythology, Bible, philosophy, Eastern and Western mysticism, art, literature, political science, and psychology. It is significant that Buber was not content with making "contributions" to some of these branches of scholarship. His aim in all his studies was to point to the one item that was to him of prime import: life as a dialogue. Here we may recall Kierkegaard's dictum: "Purity of heart is to will one thing."

Some future biographer may be tempted to face the question whether Buber's teachings of the I-Thou relationship of response, immediacy, and spontaneity of contact between man and man is a record of personal experience, or, rather, of expectation and anticipation. Buber himself speaks on several occasions of deeply meaningful personal encounters. There is also ample evidence of misunderstandings, of criticism of some of his writings and actions, which a man of Buber's sensitivity must have taken as signs of rejection, of failure to grasp the outstretched hand. He must have painfully experienced that the I-Thou relationship is a high ideal, whereas its opposite, the I-It attitude, dominates most of human behavior; that mutual trust is a rare occurrence, whereas suspicion and incomprehension are the rule; that the name of God is being used as a convenient symbol, or dismissed altogether in an antisymbolic age, whereas both the common believer and the common agnostic practice various forms of idolatry. Such a biographer will have to recognize the great loneliness in Buber's life, and value in his work his valiant defiance of pessimism, and his affirmation of a faith in God that commanded him to be faithful to man—to the last.

A common error encountered in interpretations of Buber is his designation as mystic, and the defining of his call to confrontation as a call to mystical experience. It is true that early in his career Buber went through a mystical phase, in which a feeling of exaltation over the awareness of a universal unity of being stands over and above life in the world. In this phase simple everyday life appears to obscure that which the mystic considers to be "true" life, a higher life elevated above earthly existence. But Buber radically overcame this early phase and, if anything, became an antimystic: a man committed to the everyday, a man who believes that it is precisely in this earthly existence that the Thou is to be met; that the mystical realm is an escape from human responsibility; that response is possible only in the here and now. This critical turn in Buber's life must be clearly perceived if his place in modern thought is to be seriously evaluated.

The nature of Buber's teachings makes it difficult to place

them within any given philosophical or theological category or school. Antirationalism would be just as wrong a category as mysticism, but so would be rationalism, although human reason is fully—but not solely—recognized as a source of truth. Both an element of pragmatism and many elements of humanism are present in Buber's work but neither pragmatism nor humanism can describe the range and the center of gravity of his thought. Not even the designation existentialist, or religious existentialist, fits Buber, though there are parallels between him and the thinking of Gabriel Marcel, the Christian existentialist's idea of participation.

Categories, concepts, and issues are simply useless when applied to the highly individual, tradition-conscious, yet free, exercise of Buber's philosophy. A thinker from faith: this description he accepted as adequate. But we must bear in mind that faith here does not refer to an established, conceptually circumscribed faith, but to faith which perceives individual man and humanity ever anew at a turning point of life or of history, ready for the act of encounter, and response.

N. N. Glatzer

Brandeis University
June, 1966

PROLOGUE ☉ Response

A Conversion

In my earlier years the "religious" was for me the exception. There were hours that were taken out of the course
of things. From somewhere or other the firm crust of
everyday was pierced. Then the reliable permanence of
appearances broke down; the attack which took place
burst its law asunder. "Religious experience" was the experience of an otherness which did not fit into the context of life. It could begin with something customary,
with consideration of some familiar object, but which
then became unexpectedly mysterious and uncanny,
finally lighting a way into the lightning-pierced darkness
of the mystery itself. But also, without any intermediate
stage, time could be torn apart—first the firm world's
structure then the still firmer self-assurance flew apart
and you were delivered to fulness. The "religious" lifted
you out. Over there now lay the accustomed existence
with its affairs, but here illumination and ecstasy and rap-
ture held, without time or sequence. . . .

The illegitimacy of such a division of the temporal life,
which is streaming to death and eternity and which only
in fulfilling its temporality can be fulfilled in face of these,
was brought home to me by an everyday event, an event
of judgment, judging with that sentence from closed
lips and an unmoved glance such as the ongoing course
of things loves to pronounce.

What happened was no more than that one forenoon,
after a morning of "religious" enthusiasm, I had a visit
from an unknown young man, without being there in
spirit. I certainly did not fail to let the meeting be
friendly, I did not treat him any more remissly than all
his contemporaries who were in the habit of seeking me

out about this time of day as an oracle that is ready to listen to reason. I conversed attentively and openly with him—only I omitted to guess the questions which he did not put. Later, not long after, I learned from one of his friends—he himself was no longer alive—the essential content of these questions; I learned that he had come to me not casually, but borne by destiny, not for a chat but for a decision. He had come to me, he had come in this hour. What do we expect when we are in despair and yet go to a man? Surely a presence by means of which we are told that nevertheless there is meaning.

Since then I have given up the "religious" which is nothing but the exception, extraction, exaltation, ecstasy; or it has given me up. I possess nothing but the everyday out of which I am never taken. The mystery is no longer disclosed, it has escaped or it has made its dwelling here where everything happens as it happens. I know no fulness but each mortal hour's fulness of claim and responsibility. Though far from being equal to it, yet I know that in the claim I am claimed and may respond in responsibility.

I do not know much more. If that is religion then it is just everything, simply all that is lived in its possibility of dialogue. Here is space also for religion's highest forms. As when you pray you do not thereby remove yourself from this life of yours but in your praying refer your thought to it, even though it may be in order to yield it; so too in the unprecedented and surprising, when you are called upon from above, required, chosen, empowered, sent, you with this your mortal bit of life are referred to, this moment is not extracted from it, it rests on what has been and beckons to the remainder which has still to be lived, you are not swallowed up in a fulness without obligation, you are willed for the life of communion.

Response

○

This fragile life between birth and death can nevertheless be a fulfilment—if it is a dialogue. In our life and experience we are addressed; by thought and speech and action, by producing and by influencing we are able to answer. For the most part we do not listen to the address, or we break into it with chatter. But if the word comes to us and the answer proceeds from us then human life exists, though brokenly, in the world. The kindling of the response in that "spark" of the soul, the blazing up of the response, which occurs time and again, to the unexpectedly approaching speech, we term responsibility. We practice responsibility for that realm of life allotted and entrusted to us for which we are able to respond, that is, for which we have a relation of deeds which may count—in all our inadequacy—as a proper response.

Responsibility

The idea of responsibility is to be brought back from the province of specialized ethics into that of lived life. Genuine responsibility exists only where there is real responding.

Responding to what?

To what happens to one, to what is to be seen and heard and felt. Each concrete hour allotted to the person, with its content drawn from the world and from destiny, is speech for the man who is attentive. Attentive, for no more than that is needed in order to make a beginning with the reading of the signs that are given to you.

Ethics

○

Ethical life has entered into religious life, and cannot be extracted from it. There is no responsibility unless there is One to whom one is responsible, for there is no response where there is no address. In the last resort, religious life means concreteness itself, the whole concreteness of life without reduction, grasped dialogically, included in the dialogue.

Reality

With all deference to the world continuum of space and time I know as a living truth only concrete world reality which is constantly, in every moment, reached out to me. I can separate it into its component parts, I can compare them and distribute them into groups of similar phenomena, I can derive them from earlier and reduce them to simpler phenomena; and when I have done all this I have not touched my concrete world reality. Inseparable, incomparable, irreducible, now, happening once only, it gazes upon me with an awesome look.

GOD · I

Who Speaks?

In the signs of life which happens to us we are addressed. Who speaks?

It would not avail us to give for reply the word "God," if we do not give it out of that decisive hour of personal existence when we had to forget everything we imagined we knew of God, when we dared to keep nothing handed down or learned or self-contrived, no shred of knowledge, and were plunged into the night.

When we rise out of it into the new life and there begin to receive the signs, what can we know of that which—of Him who gives them to us? Only what we experience from time to time from the signs themselves. If we name the speaker of this speech God, then it is always the God of a moment.

Absolute Personality

He who loves God loves the ideal and loves God more than the ideal. He knows himself to be loved by God, not by the ideal, not by an idea, but by Him exactly whom ideality cannot grasp, namely, by that absolute personality we call God. Can this be taken to mean that God "is" a personality? The absolute character of His personality, that paradox of paradoxes, prohibits any such statement. It only means that God loves as a personality and that He wishes to be loved like a personality. And if He was not a person in Himself, He, so to speak, became one in creating Man, in order to love man and be loved by him—in order to love me and be loved by me.

God and World

Only he who learns to love men one by one reaches, in his relation to heaven, God as the God of all the world. He who does not love the world can only refer, in his relationship to God, to an equally solitary God or to the God of his own soul. For he learns to love the God of the universe, the God who loves His world, only in the measure in which he himself learns to love the world.

Spirit and Nature

☉

One does not serve God with the spirit only, but with the whole of his nature, without any subtractions. There is not one realm of the spirit and another of nature; there is only the growing kingdom of God. God is not spirit, but what we call spirit and what we call nature hail equally from the God who is beyond and equally unconditioned by both, and whose kingdom reaches its fulness in the complete unity of spirit and nature.

Wholeness Alone

Whoever desires to confine himself to an emotional relationship to God, without perceiving the living world about him and without recognizing the life therein, robs mankind of what is due to it and thus surely also of what belongs to it. And he who exercises his spirit only and thinks about nothing else, who is attached to God and the world only by the external ties of traditionally transmitted religion and morals, but knows neither piety nor goodness, will pretty soon lose even that weak hold which those external ties provide. Whatever is isolated is confusing. Wholeness alone is reliable and leads man to salvation.

Not What But How

○

In the unconditionality of his deed man experiences his communion with God. God is an unknown Being beyond this world only for the indolent, the decisionless, the lethargic, the man enmeshed in his own designs; for the one who chooses, who decides, who is aflame with his goal, who is unconditioned, God is the closest, the most familiar Being that man, through his own action, realizes ever anew, experiencing thereby the mystery of mysteries. Whether God is "transcendent" or "immanent" does not depend on Him; it depends on man. . . .

The truth men do is not a What but a How. Not the matter of a deed determines its truth but the manner in which it is carried out: in human conditionality, or in divine unconditionality. Whether a deed will peter out in the outer courtyard, in the realm of things, or whether it will penetrate into the Holy of Holies is determined not by its content but by the power of decision which brought it about, and by the sanctity of intent which dwells in it. Any deed, even one numbered among the most profane, is holy when it is performed in holiness, in unconditionality.

Symbols

☉

Dogmas and rules are merely the result, subject to change, of the human mind's attempt to make comprehensible, by a symbolic order of the knowable and doable, the working of the unconditional it experiences within itself. Primary reality is constituted by the effect of the unconditional upon the human mind which, sustained by the force of its own vision, unflinchingly faces the supreme power. Man's mind thus experiences the unconditional as that great something which is set over against it, as the Thou as such. By creating symbols, the mind comprehends what is in itself incomprehensible: thus, in symbol and adage, the illimitable God reveals Himself to the human mind, which gathers the flowing universal currents into the receptacle of an affirmation that declares the Lord reigns in this and in no other way. Or man's mind captures a flash of the original source of light in the mirror of some rule which declares that the Lord must be served in this and in no other way. But neither symbol nor adage makes man unworthy or untrue; they are rather forms the unconditional itself creates within man's mind which, at this particular time, has not yet developed into a more effective tool. "For the divine wishes to evolve within mankind." In mankind's great ages, the divine, in invisible becoming, outgrows old symbolisms and blossoms forth in new ones. The symbol becomes ever more internalized, moves ever closer to the heart, and is ever more deeply submerged in life itself; and the man who five thousand years ago saw it in the stars, sees it today in the eyes of a friend. It is not God who changes, only theophany—the manifestation of the divine in man's symbol-creating mind: until no symbol is adequate any longer, and none is needed, and life itself, in the miracle of man's being with man, becomes a symbol —until God is actually present when one man clasps the hand of another.

Transcendence

The personal manifestation of the divine is not decisive for the genuineness of religion. What is decisive is that I relate myself to the divine as to Being which is over against me, though not over against me alone. Complete inclusion of the divine in the sphere of the human self abolishes its divinity. It is not necessary to know something about God in order really to believe in Him: many true believers know how to talk to God but not about Him. If one dares to turn toward the unknown God, to go to meet Him, to call to Him, reality is present. He who refuses to limit God to the transcendent has a fuller conception of Him than he who does so limit Him. But he who confines God within the immanent means something other than Him.

Dualism

○

We shall accomplish nothing at all if we divide our world and our life into two domains: one in which God's command is paramount, the other governed exclusively by the laws of economics, politics, and the "simple self-assertion" of the group. Such dualism is far more ominous than the naturalism I spoke of before. Stopping one's ears so as not to hear the voice from above is breaking the connection between existence and the meaning of existence. But he who hears the voice and sets a limit to the area beyond which its rule shall not extend is not merely moving away from God, like the person who refuses to listen; he is standing up directly against Him.

Imitatio

Man cannot "be like unto God," but with all the inadequacy of each of his days, he can follow God at all times, using the capacity he has on that particular day—and if he has used the capacity of that day to the full, he has done enough. This is not a mere act of faith; it is an entering into the life that has to be lived on that day with all the active fulness of a created person.

Unity

○

We "unify" God, when living and dying we profess His unity; we do not unite ourselves with Him. The God in whom we believe, to whom we are pledged, does not unite with human substance on earth. But the very fact that we do not imagine that we can unite with Him enables us the more ardently to hope "that the world be perfected under the kingship of the Almighty."

The Secret and the Manifest

❍

The secret of God which stood over Job's tent (Job 29:4), before it grew terrifyingly into his suffering and questioning, can only be fathomed by suffering, not by questioning, and man is equally forbidden to question and to follow these secret ways of God. But God's handiwork, His revealed way of working, has been opened before us and set up for us as a pattern. . . .

But where are the revealed ways of God's working revealed?

Just at the beginning of the wandering through the desert; just at the height of Job's trial; just in the midst of the terror of the other, the incomprehensible, ununderstandable works; just from out of the secret. God does not show mercy and grace alone to us; it is terrible when His hand falls on us, and what then happens to us does not somehow find a place beside mercy and grace, it does not belong to the same category as these: the ultimate does not belong here to the "attribute of stern justice"—it is beyond all attributes. It is indeed the secret, and it is not for us to inquire into it. But just in this quality of God's is His "handiwork" manifested to us. Only when the secret no longer stands over our tent, but breaks it, do we learn to know God's intercourse with us. And we learn to imitate God.

Images

Whether or not we know it, what we really mean when we say that a god is dead is that the images of God vanish, and that therefore an image which up to now was regarded and worshipped as God, can no longer be so regarded and so worshipped. For what we call gods are nothing but images of God and must suffer the fate of such images. But Nietzsche manifestly wished to say something different, and that something different is terribly wrong in a way characteristic of our time. For it means confusing an image, confusing one of the many images of God that are born and perish, with the real God whose reality men could never shake with any one of these images, no matter what forms they might honestly invent for the objects of their particular adoration.

Time after time, the images must be broken, the iconoclasts must have their way. For the iconoclast is the soul of man which rebels against having an image that can no longer be believed in, elevated above the heads of man as a thing that demands to be worshipped. In their longing for a god, men try again and again to set up a greater, a more genuine and more just image, which is intended to be more glorious than the last and only proves the more unsatisfactory.

The commandment, "Thou shalt not make unto thee an image," means at the same time, "Thou canst not make an image." This does not, of course, refer merely to sculptured or painted images, but to our fantasy, to all the power of our imagination as well. But man is forced time and again to make images, and forced to destroy them when he realizes that he has not succeeded.

The images topple, but the voice is never silenced. . . .

The voice speaks in the guise of everything that happens, in the guise of all world events; it speaks to the men of all generations, makes demands upon them, and summons them to accept their responsibility. . . . It is of the utmost importance not to lose one's openness. But to be open means not to shut out the voice—call it what you will. It does not matter what you call it. All that matters is that you hear it.

The Word and the Name

○

"God" is the most heavy-laden of all human words. None has·become so soiled, so mutilated. Just for this reason I may not abandon it. Generations of men have laid the burden of their anxious lives upon this word and weighed it to the ground; it lies in the dust and bears their whole burden. The races of man with their religious factions have torn the word to pieces; they have killed for it and died for it, and it bears their finger-marks and their blood. Where might I find a word like it to describe the highest! If I took the purest, most sparkling concept from the inner treasure-chamber of the philosophers, I could only capture thereby an unbinding product of thought. I could not capture the presence of Him whom the generations of men have honored and degraded with their awesome living and dying. I do indeed mean Him whom the hell-tormented and heaven-storming generations of men mean. Certainly, they draw caricatures and write "God" underneath; they murder one another and say "in God's name."

But when all madness and delusion fall to dust, when they stand over against Him in the loneliest darkness and no longer say "He, He" but rather sigh "Thou," shout "Thou," all of them the one word, and when they then add God, is it not the real God whom they all implore, the One Living God, the God of the children of man? Is it not He who hears them? And just for this reason is not the word God, the word of appeal, the word which has become a name, consecrated in all human tongues for all times? We must esteem those who interdict it because they rebel against the injustice and wrong which are so readily re-ferred to "God" for authorization. But we may not give it up. How understandable it is that some suggest we should remain silent about the "last things" for a time in order that the misused words may be redeemed! But they are not to be redeemed thus. We cannot cleanse the word God and we cannot make it whole; but, defiled and mutilated as it is, we can raise it from the ground and set it over an hour of great concern.

God as a Person

○

The description of God as a Person is indispensable for
everyone who like myself means by "God" not a principle
(although mystics like Eckhart sometimes identify Him
with "Being") and like myself means by "God" not an idea
(although philosophers like Plato at times could hold that
He was this): but who rather means by "God," as I do,
Him who—whatever else he may be—enters into a direct
relation with us men in creative, revealing, and redeeming
acts, and thus makes it possible for us to enter into a direct
relation with Him. This ground and meaning of our existence constitutes a mutuality, arising again and again, such
as can subsist only between persons. The concept of personal being is indeed completely incapable of declaring
what God's essential being is, but it is both permitted and
necessary to say that God is *also* a Person.

Spinoza

❍

Spinoza undertook to take from God His being open to man's address. One cannot suppose that his *deus sive natura* is "another God." He himself meant no other than Him whom he had addressed as a boy, Him who is the very origin and goal of all being; he only wanted to purify Him from the stain of being open to address. A God who was capable of being addressed was not pure enough, not great enough, not divine enough for him. The fundamental error of Spinoza was that he imagined that in the teaching of Israel only the teaching that God is a person was to be found and he opposed it as a diminution of divinity. But the truth of the teaching is that God is *also* a person, and this is, in contrast to all impersonal, unaddressable "purity" of God, an augmentation of divinity.

The tendency of the Western spirit toward monological life was decisively forwarded by Spinoza—and thereby the crisis of the spirit in general, since in the air of monological life it must gloriously wither.

I AND THOU ∘ II

Limits

◔

Human life and humanity come into being in genuine meetings. There man learns not merely that he is limited by man, cast upon his own finitude, partialness, need of completion, but his own relation to truth is heightened by the other's different relation to the same truth—different in accordance with his individuation, and destined to take seed and grow differently. Men need, and it is granted to them, to confirm one another in their individual being by means of genuine meetings. But beyond this they need, and it is granted to them, to see that the truth, which the soul gains by its struggle, is flashing up for the others, the brothers, in a different way, and equally confirmed.

The Primary Word

○

The primary word I-Thou can be spoken only with the whole being. Concentration and fusion into the whole being can never take place through my agency, nor can it ever take place without me. I become through my relation to the Thou; as I become I, I say Thou.

All real living is meeting.

Obstacles

○

The relation to the Thou is direct. No system of concepts, no foreknowledge, and no fancy intervene between I and Thou. The memory itself is transformed, as it plunges out of its isolation into the unity of the whole. No set purpose, no greed, and no anticipation intervene between I and Thou. Desire itself is transformed as it plunges out of its dream into the appearance. Every means is an obstacle. Only when every means has collapsed does the meeting come about.

It-Thou

In all the seriousness of truth, hear this: without It man cannot live. But he who lives with It alone is not a man.

How powerful is the unbroken world of It, and how delicate are the appearances of the Thou!

The Eternal Thou

○

The extended lines of relations meet in the eternal Thou.

Every particular Thou is a glimpse through to the eternal Thou; by means of every particular Thou the primary word addresses the eternal Thou.

Realization vs. Reflection

○

Meeting with God does not come to man in order that he may concern himself with God, but in order that he may realize meaning in the world. All revelation is summons and sending. But again and again man brings about, instead of realization, a reflection to Him who reveals: he wishes to concern himself with God instead of with the world. Only, in such a reflection, he is no longer confronted by a Thou, he can do nothing but establish an It-God in the realm of things, believe that he knows of God as of an It, and so speak about Him. Just as the "self"-seeking man, instead of directly living something or other, a perception or an affection, reflects about his perceptive or reflective I, and thereby misses the truth of the event, so the man who seeks God (though for the rest he gets on very well with the self-seeker in the one soul), instead of allowing the gift to work itself out, reflects about the Giver—and misses both.

God Needs You

You know always in your heart that you need God more than everything; but do you not know too that God needs you—in the fulness of His eternity needs you? How would man exist, how would you exist, if God did not need him, did not need you? You need God, in order to be—and God needs you, for the very meaning of your life.

The world is not divine sport, it is divine destiny. There is divine meaning in the life of the world, of man, of human persons, of you and of me.

Creation happens to us, burns itself into us, recasts us in burning—we tremble and are faint, we submit. We take part in creation, meet the Creator, reach out to Him, helpers and companions.

Thinking

○

If we are serious about thinking between I and Thou, then it is not enough to cast our thoughts toward the other subject of thought framed by thought. We should also, with the thinking, precisely with the thinking, live toward the other man, who is not framed by thought but bodily present before us; we should live toward his concrete life. We should live not toward another thinker of whom we wish to know nothing beyond his thinking but, even if the other is a thinker, toward his bodily life over and above his thinking —rather, toward his person, to which, to be sure, the activity of thinking also belongs.

The Third Alternative

In the most powerful moments of dialogic, where in truth "deep calls unto deep," it becomes unmistakably clear that it is not the wand of the individual or of the social, but of a third which draws the circle round the happening. On the far side of the subjective, on this side of the objective, on the narrow ridge, where I and Thou meet, there is the realm of "between."

This reality, whose disclosure has begun in our time, shows the way, leading beyond individualism and collectivism, for the life decision of future generations. Here the genuine third alternative is indicated, the knowledge of which will help to bring about the genuine person again and to establish genuine community.

In Our Age

In our age the I-It relation, gigantically swollen, has usurped, practically uncontested, the mastery and the rule. The I of this relation, an I that possesses all, makes all, succeeds with all, this I that is unable to say Thou, unable to meet a being essentially, is the lord of the hour. This selfhood that has become omnipotent, with all the It around it, can naturally acknowledge neither God nor any genuine absolute which manifests itself to men as of non-human origin. It steps in between and shuts off from us the light of heaven.

Hope

○

The hope for this hour depends upon the renewal of dialogical immediacy between men. But let us look beyond the pressing need, the anxiety and care of this hour. Let us see this need in connection with the great human way. Then we shall recognize that immediacy is injured not only between man and man, but also between the being called man and the source of his existence. At its core the conflict between the mistrust and trust of man conceals the conflict between the mistrust and trust of eternity. If our mouths succeed in genuinely saying "thou," then, after long silence and stammering, we shall have addressed our eternal "Thou" anew. Reconciliation leads toward reconciliation.

FAITH ◯ III

Into My Very Life

○

Real faith begins when the dictionary is put down, when you are done with it. What occurs to me says something to me, but what it says to me cannot be revealed by any esoteric information; for it has never been said before nor is it composed of sounds that have ever been said. It can neither be interpreted nor translated, I can have it neither explained nor displayed; it is not a what at all, it is said into my very life; it is no experience that can be remembered independently of the situation, it remains the address of that moment and cannot be isolated, it remains the question of a questioner and will have its answer.

Meaning

The religious essence in every religion can be found in its highest certainty. That is the certainty that the meaning of existence is open and accessible in the actual lived concrete, not above the struggle with reality but in it.

That meaning is open and accessible in the actual lived concrete does not mean it is to be won and possessed through any type of analytic or synthetic investigation or through any type of reflection upon the lived concrete. Meaning is to be experienced in living action and suffering itself, in the unreduced immediacy of the moment. Of course, he who aims at the experiencing of experience will necessarily miss the meaning, for he destroys the spontaneity of the mystery. Only he reaches the meaning who stands firm, without holding back or reservation, before the whole might of reality and answers it in a living way. He is ready to confirm with his life the meaning which he has attained.

Every religious utterance is a vain attempt to do justice to the meaning which has been attained. All religious expression is only an intimation of its attainment. . . . The meaning is found through the engagement of one's own person; it only reveals itself as one takes part in its revelation.

Fear of God

All religious reality begins with what Biblical religion calls the "fear of God." It comes when our existence between birth and death becomes incomprehensible and uncanny, when all security is shattered through the mystery. This is not the relative mystery of that which is inaccessible only to the present state of human knowledge and is hence in principle discoverable. It is the essential mystery, the inscrutableness of which belongs to its very nature; it is the unknowable. Through this dark gate (which is only a gate and not, as some theologians assert, a dwelling) the believing man steps forth into the everyday which is henceforth hallowed as the place in which he has to live with the mystery. He steps forth directed and assigned to the concrete, contextual situations of his existence. That he henceforth accepts the situation as given him by the Giver is what Biblical religion calls the "fear of God."

The Deed

○

Religiosity is man's urge to establish a living communion with the unconditioned; it is man's will to realize the unconditioned through his deed, and to establish it in his world. Genuine religiosity, therefore, has nothing in common with the fancies of romantic hearts, or the self-pleasure of aestheticizing souls, or the clever mental exercises of a practiced intellectuality. Genuine religiosity is doing. It wants to sculpt the unconditioned out of the matter of this world. The countenance of God reposes, invisible, in an earthen block; it must be wrought, carved out of it. To be engaged in this work means to be religious—nothing else.

Men's life, open to our influence as is no other thing in this world, is the task apportioned to us in its most inward immediacy. Here, as nowhere else, there is given to us a formless mass, to be in-formed by us with the divine. The community of men is as yet only a projected opus that is waiting for us; a chaos we must put in order; a Diaspora we must gather in; a conflict to which we must bring reconciliation. But this we can accomplish only if, in the natural context of a life shared with others, everyone of us, each in his own place, will perform the just, the unifying, the in-forming deed: for God does not want to be believed in, to be debated and defended by us, but simply to be realized through us.

The Ethical Aspect

The essence of the relationship between the ethical and the religious cannot be determined by comparing the teachings of ethics and religion. One must rather penetrate into that area within each sphere where they become solidified in a concrete, personal situation. Thus it is the factual moral decision of the individual on the one hand and his factual relationship to the Absolute on the other that concerns us. In both cases it is not a mere faculty of the person that is involved, whether it be his thought or his feeling or his will, but the totality of these faculties, and more than that, the whole man. A third sphere overlying these two is not given us; we can only let the two confront each other, and in such a way that in this meeting each of them determines its relationship to the other. If from the point of view of the religious we look in such concreteness at the relation between the two spheres, we shall see its strong tendency to send forth its rays into the whole life of the person, effecting a comprehensive structural change. Living religiousness wishes to bring forth living ethos. Something essentially different meets our view if we seek to examine the connection between the two fields from the standpoint of the ethical. The man who seeks distinction and decision in his own soul cannot draw from it, from his soul, absoluteness for his scale of values. Only out of a personal relationship with the Absolute can the absoluteness of the ethical co-ordinates arise without which there is no complete awareness of self. Even when the individual calls an absolute criterion handed down by religious tradition his own, it must be reforged in the fire of the truth of his personal essential relation to the Absolute if it is to win true validity. But always it is the religious which bestows, the ethical which receives.

Direction

Nothing is unholy in itself, nothing is in itself evil. What we call evil is only the directionless plunging and storming of the sparks in need of redemption. It is "passion"—the very same power which, when it has been endowed with direction, the one direction, brings forth the good in truth, the true service, the hallowing. Thus there no longer exist side by side in the soul of man the worldly and the spiritual, qualitatively sundered, there are now only power and direction. He who divides his life between God and the world, through giving the world "what is its" to save for God "what is His," denies God the service He demands, the giving of direction to all power, the hallowing of the everyday in the world and the soul.

In the Hasidic message the separation between "life in God" and "life in the world," the primal evil of all "religion," is overcome in genuine, concrete unity. But a rejoinder is also given here to the false overcoming of the separation through the abstract dissolution of the difference between God and the world. Hasidism preserves undiminished God's distance from and superiority to the world in which He nonetheless dwells. In this distance Hasidism sets the undivided wholeness of human life in its full meaning: that it should receive the world from God and act on the world for the sake of God. Bound to the world, receiving and acting, man stands directly before God—not "man" rather, but this particular man, you, I.

Prayer

○

We call prayer in the pregnant sense of the term that speech of man to God which, whatever else is asked, ultimately asks for the manifestation of the divine presence, for this presence's becoming dialogically perceivable. The single presupposition of a genuine state of prayer is thus the readiness of the whole man for this presence, simple turned-towardness, unreserved spontaneity.

Biblical Humanism

○

The *humanitas* which speaks from this Book [the Bible] today, as it has always done, is the unity of human life under one divine direction which divides right from wrong and truth from lies as unconditionally as the words of the Creator divided light from darkness. It is true that we are not able to live in perfect justice, and in order to preserve the community of man, we are often compelled to accept wrongs in decisions concerning the community. But what matters is that in every hour of decision we are aware of our responsibility and summon our conscience to weigh exactly how much is necessary to preserve the community, and accept just so much and no more; that we do not interpret the demands of a will to power as a demand made by life itself; that we do not make a practice of setting aside a certain sphere in which God's command does not hold, but regard those actions as against his command, forced on us by the exigencies of the hour as painful sacrifices; that we do not salve, or let others salve, our conscience when we make decisions concerning public life, but struggle with destiny in fear and trembling lest it burden us with greater guilt than we are compelled to assume. This trembling of the magnetic needle which points the direction notwithstanding—this is Biblical *humanitas*. The men in the Bible are sinners like ourselves, but there is one sin they do not commit, our arch-sin: they do not dare confine God to a circumscribed space or division of life, to "religion." They have not the insolence to draw boundaries around God's commandments and say to Him: "Up to this point, You are sovereign, but beyond these bounds begins the sovereignty of science or society or the state."

Religious Humanism

○

Of decisive importance for the problem of an authentic religious humanism in our time is the realization that the truly human element and religious experience have their roots in the same soil: encounter. In fact, the fundamental religious experience as such may be regarded as the ultimate climax of the encounter's reality. This doubtlessly holds true for the religious life of the area bordered in the East by the Arabian Sea and in the West by the Pacific Ocean. It seems, however, that even far beyond this area, that indeed throughout all of mankind, the encounter with the incomprehensible constitutes the beginning of any personal religious experience, recurring over and over again even within this experience, and confirming as well as renewing it.

With this in mind, we can envision a modern religious humanism which combines the human element and religiosity in such a way that they do not merely dwell side by side but permeate each other.

Now, one may object to my use of the adjective "modern," on the grounds that it is precisely in our time that very little of such religious humanism can be discerned. And it would indeed seem that today, more than at any other time, a certain type of man predominates, a man who would rather observe and use the human beings he encounters in the course of his life than turn toward them with his soul and offer his deed. But in this very "today" there has arisen a powerful motivation toward a new and genuine religious humanism. I mean the crisis of mankind that is threatened with destruction. I mean the technology that has lost all sense of direction; the uncontrolled prevalence of means that no longer need to be justified by any ends;

and I mean man's deliberate enslavement in the service of the split atom. More and more members of the emergent and still pliable generation are becoming aware of what is in the making. And their awareness, augmented day by day, the perception of a crisis, awakens in them the only counterbalancing force which may succeed in setting up, once again, goals—great, shining ends to subjugate the insurgent means. It is this counterbalancing force that I call the new religious humanism.

The Danger of "Religion"

The communion of man with God not only has its place in the world, but also its subject. God speaks to man in the things and beings that He sends him in life; man answers through his action in relation to just these things and beings. All specific service of God has its meaning only in the ever-renewed preparation and hallowing for this communion with God in the world. But there is a danger, in fact, the utmost danger and temptation of man, that something becomes detached from the human side of this communion and makes itself independent, rounds itself off, seemingly perfects itself to reciprocity, yet puts itself in the place of real communion. The primal danger of man is "religion."

That which thus makes itself independent can be the forms in which man hallows the world for God, the "cultic-sacramental." Now they no longer mean the consecration of the lived everyday, but its amputation; life in the world and the service of God run side by side without connection. But the "God" of this service is no longer God; it is the semblance—the real partner of the communion is no longer there; the gestures of intercourse fall on the empty air.

The Existing God

○

If philosophy is set in contrast to religion, what is meant by religion is not the massive fulness of statements, concepts, and activities that one customarily describes by this name and that men sometimes long for more than for God. Religion is essentially the act of holding fast to God. And that does not mean holding fast to an image that one has made of God, nor even holding fast to the faith in God that one has conceived. It means holding fast to the existing God. The earth would not hold fast to its conception of the sun (if it had one) nor to its connection with it, but to the sun itself.

Reciprocity

○

Philosophy errs in thinking of religion as founded in a noetic act, even if an inadequate one, and in therefore regarding the essence of religion as the knowledge of an object which is indifferent to being known. As a result, philosophy understands faith as an affirmation of truth lying somewhere between clear knowledge and confused opinion. Religion, on the other hand, insofar as it speaks of knowledge at all, does not understand it as a noetic relation of a thinking subject to a neutral object of thought, but rather as mutual contact, as the genuinely reciprocal meeting in the fulness of life between one active existence and another. Similarly, it understands faith as the entrance into this reciprocity, as binding oneself in relationship with an undemonstrable and unprovable, yet even so, in relationship, knowable Being, from whom all meaning comes.

Knowledge

◑

Religion is not allowed, even in the face of the most self-confident pride of philosophy, to remain blind to philosophy's great engagement. To this engagement necessarily belongs the actual, ever-recurring renunciation of the original relational bond, of the reality which takes place between I and Thou, of the spontaneity of the moment. Religion must know knowledge not only as a need but also as a duty of man. It must know that history moves along the way of this need and duty, that, Biblically speaking, the eating of the tree of knowledge leads out of Paradise but into the world.

Reading the Bible

The man of today has no access to a sure and solid faith, nor can it be made accessible to him. If he examines himself seriously, he knows this and may not delude himself further. But he is not denied the possibility of holding himself open to faith. If he is really serious, he too can open up to this book and let its rays strike him where they will. He can give himself up and submit to the test without preconceived notions and without reservations. He can absorb the Bible with all his strength, and wait to see what will happen to him, whether he will not discover within himself a new and unbiased approach to this or that element in the book. But to this end, he must read the Scriptures as though they were something entirely unfamiliar, as though they had not been set before him ready-made, at school and after in the light of "religious" and "scientific" certainties; as though he has not been confronted all his life with sham concepts and sham statements which cited the Bible as their authority. He must face the book with a new attitude as something new. He must yield to it, withhold nothing of his being, and let whatever will occur between himself and it. He does not know which of its sayings and images will overwhelm him and mold him, from where the spirit will ferment and enter into him, to incorporate itself anew in his body. But he holds himself open. He does not believe anything a priori; he does not disbelieve anything a priori. He reads aloud the words written in the book in front of him; he hears the word he utters and it reaches him. Nothing is prejudged. The current of time flows on, and the contemporary character of this man becomes itself a receiving vessel.

Spirituality

○

I am deeply distressed to find a great number of our young people sharing a prejudice against spirituality—even though I quite understand how this came about. It is not difficult to comprehend why many now guard themselves against having faith or confidence in the spirit. For during the past decades the race of man has not, by and large, fared well at the hands of the spirit. For the spirit was not simply silent; it spoke falsely at junctures when it should have had an important voice in history, when it should have told the truth about what was being done or not being done to those who were making or seemed to be making history. On frequent occasions the spirit consented to be a tool when it should have acted on its own in the capacity of judge and censor. Then again, it has repeatedly retired to a magnificent isolated kingdom of its own, poised high above the world in the realm of circling ideas. Whenever the spirit has done so, it has sacrificed the very factor which makes it legitimate, particularly in crises: its readiness to expose itself to reality, to prove and express itself in reality.

To Youth

○

We are not concerned with imposing religion upon youth, but with awakening its own latent religion; that means: its willingness to confront unwaveringly the impact of the unconditional. We must not preach to youth that God's revelation becomes manifest in only one, and no other, way, but show them that nothing is incapable of becoming a receptacle of revelation; must not proclaim to youth that God can be served by only one, and no other, act, but make clear to them that every deed is hallowed if it radiates the spirit of unity; must not ask them to avow as exclusively binding in their lives only that which emanated at some hour of the past, but affirm for them that "each man has his hour" when the gate opens for him and the word becomes audible to him. We who stand in awe of that which is unknowable do not want to transmit to youth a knowledge of God's nature and work. We who consider life as more divine than laws and rules do not want to regulate the life of youth by laws and rules attributed to God. We want to help youth not to bypass its destiny, not to miss its metaphysical self-discovery by being asleep, and to respond nobly when it senses within itself the power of the unconditional. By so doing, we do not diminish the openness of youth, but promote and deeply affirm it; do not curtain any of its windows, but let it, as if it has become all eyes, absorb the all-encompassing view; do not shut off any road, but make it easier for youth to see that all roads, if walked in truth and consecration, lead to the threshold of the divine.

One Front

○

There is, it seems to me, a front—only seldom perceived by those who compose it—that cuts across all the fronts of the hour, both the external and the internal. There they stand, ranged side by side, the men of real conviction who are found in all groups, all parties, all peoples, yet who know little or nothing of one another from group to group, from party to party, from people to people. As different as the goals are in one place and in another, it is still one front, for they are all engaged in the one fight for human truth. But human truth is nothing other than the faithfulness of man to the one truth that he cannot possess, that he can only serve, his fidelity to the truth of God. Remaining true to the truth as much as he can, he strives toward his goal. The goals are different, very different, but if each way has been trod in truth, the lines leading to these goals intersect, extended beyond them, in the truth of God. Those who stand on the cross-front, those who know nothing of one another, have to do with one another.

Courage and Love

The relation of the spirit to the elemental forces and urges must not be interpreted from the point of view of pure thought. An attempt at interpretation must consider the influence of the spirit upon life. But—regardless of what it may call itself or be called at any given moment—the spirit which is not content in the area of thought and expresses itself in all of life becomes manifest as the power of faith. In the domain of the human soul, it appears as faithful courage and faithful love. Based on the power of faith, the spirit exerts its influence upon the world through its agents, courage and love. These constitute its power which may well govern the elemental forces because it has known them from the earliest times, and knows what is their due. Though in one historical era after another the spirit may seem dethroned and exiled, it does not lose its power. Again and again, unexpectedly and unpredictably, it causes what is intrinsic in the course of history through its agents, faithful courage and faithful love.

MAN ◉ IV

Man—An Audacity of Life

Because man is the sole living creature known to us in whom the category of possibility is so to speak embodied, and whose reality is incessantly enveloped by possibilities, he alone amongst them all needs confirmation. Every animal is fixed in its this-being, its modifications are preordained, and when it changes into a caterpillar and into a chrysalis its very metamorphosis is a boundary; in everything together it remains exactly what it is, therefore it can need no confirmation; it would, indeed, be an absurdity for someone to say to it, or for it to say to itself: You may be what you are. Man as man is an audacity of life, undetermined and unfixed; he therefore requires confirmation, and he can naturally only receive this as individual man, in that others and he himself confirm him in his being-this-man. Again and again the Yes must be spoken to him, from the look of the confidant and from the stirrings of his own heart, to liberate him from the dread of abandonment, which is a foretaste of death.

The Threefold Relation

○

By virtue of his nature and his situation man has a threefold living relation. He can bring his nature and situation to full reality in his life if all his living relations become essential. And he can let elements of his nature and situation remain in unreality by letting only single living relations become essential, while considering and treating the others as unessential.

Man's threefold living relation is, first, his relation to the world and to things; second, his relation to men—both to individuals and to the many; third, his relation to the mystery of being—which is dimly apparent through all this but infinitely transcends it—which the philosopher calls the Absolute and the believer calls God, and which cannot in fact be eliminated from the situation even by a man who rejects both designations.

Independence

The presupposition for the connection existing between the ethical and the religious is the basic view that man, while created by God, was established by Him in an independence which has since remained undiminished. In this independence he stands over against God. So man takes part with full freedom and spontaneity in the dialogue between the two which forms the essence of existence. That this is so despite God's unlimited power and knowledge is just that which constitutes the mystery of man's creation.

We

○

For the typical man of today the flight from responsible personal existence has singularly polarized. Since he is not willing to answer for the genuineness of his existence, he flees either into the general collective which takes from him his responsibility or into the attitude of a self who has to account to no one but himself and finds the great general indulgence in the security of being identical with the Self of being. Even if this attitude is turned into a deepened contemplation of existence, it remains a flight from the leaping fire.

The clearest mark of this kind of man is that he cannot really listen to the voice of another; in all his hearing, as in all his seeing, he mixes observation. The other is not the man whose claim stands over against his own in equal right; the other is only his object. But he who existentially knows no Thou will never succeed in knowing a We.

In our age, in which the true meaning of every word is encompassed by delusion and falsehood, and the original intention of the human glance is stifled by tenacious mistrust, it is of decisive importance to find again the genuineness of speech and existence as We. This is no longer a matter which concerns the small circles that have been so important in the essential history of man; this is a matter of leavening the human race in all places with genuine We-ness. Man will not persist in existence if he does not learn anew to persist in it as a genuine We.

Perfected Relation

○

With the awakening of personhood awakes the dissatisfaction with the whole natural receiving of what is allotted and with it the "free" extra allowance that *Homo ludens* treats himself to. But at the same time there arises in the person, binding itself in the most remarkable way with this dissatisfaction, that which I call the longing for perfected relation or for perfection in the relation. The imperfect relations belong to the world of needing and getting or to its play-annexes. But the human person desires more than this. He does not content himself with the measure and degree of the development of relations that are required for the mastering of the needs of daily life and for entering into the regulated freedoms of play: the higher wish appears. In it the genuineness of the person becomes manifest.

The sphere of using and getting, is here [in love] not merely to be understood psychophysically, in the sex act and the movements playing around it, but also sociologically, in the continuity of marriage and family; so far, indeed, the animal and man reach a common province. But the essential love of two beings that is added to that province, that which penetrates both the contact of the sexes and the founding of the generations and transforms them into fully human existence, stems out of another realm in which the dissatisfaction with the world of using and getting and the longing for the perfection of relation blend. . . . In all love to man—I mean, naturally, not the performance of duty that takes place in so-called neighbor love, but the earnest affirmation of the human person as such—there shines forth perfected relation.

Truth

◑

Is there a truth we can possess? Can we appropriate it?
There certainly is none we can pick up and put in our
pocket. But the individual can have an honest and uncom-
promising attitude toward the truth; he can have a legitimate relationship to truth and hold and uphold it all his life.
A man may serve Truth for seven years and yet another
seven and still not win her, but his relationship has become
more genuine and true, more and more truth itself. He cannot achieve this relationship to truth without breaking
through his conditionality. He cannot shed it altogether;
that is never within his power. But he can, at least, sense
something of unconditionality—he can breathe its air. From
that time on, this "something of" will quicken his relationship to the truth. Human truth becomes real when one tries
to translate one's relationship to truth into the reality of
one's life. And human truth can be communicated only if
one throws one's self into the process and answers for it
with one's self.

One Lives It

Truth in the world of man is not to be found as the content of knowledge, but only as human existence. One does not reflect upon it, one does not express it, one does not perceive it, but one lives it and receives it as life.

Totality

Spirit is not a late bloom on the tree Man, but what constitutes man. The fact that man is a unit of substance which cannot be grasped if we regard it merely as a phenomenon of nature, the fact that there is a category of existence called Man, is based on the particular human consciousness. Spirit, then, is not just one human faculty among others. It is man's totality that has become consciousness, the totality which comprises and integrates all his capacities, powers, qualities, and urges. When a man thinks, he thinks with his entire body; spiritual man thinks even with his fingertips. Spiritual life is nothing but the existence of man, insofar as he possesses that true human conscious totality, which is not the result of development; it goes back to the origin of mankind, though it may unfold differently in different individuals.

Circumstances

○

Unmistakably men are more and more determined by "circumstances." Not only the absolute mass but also the relative might of social objectives is growing. As one determined partially by them the individual stands in each moment before concrete reality which wishes to reach out to him and receive an answer from him; laden with the situation he meets new situations. And yet in all the multiplicity and complexity he has remained Adam. Even now a real decision is made in him, whether he faces the speech of God articulated to him in things and events—or escapes. And a creative glance toward his fellow-creature can at times suffice for response.

Man is in a growing measure sociologically determined. But this growing should involve the maturing of a charge. . . . It is a matter of renouncing the pantechnic mania or habit with its easy "mastery" of every situation; of taking everything up into the might of dialogue of the genuine life, from the trivial mysteries of everyday to the majesty of destructive fate.

Nothing But the Image

○

The question which is always being brought forward—
"To where, to what, must we educate?"—misunderstands
the situation. Only times which know a figure of general
validity—the Christian, the gentleman, the citizen—know
an answer to that question, not necessarily in words, but by
pointing with the finger to the figure which rises clear in
the air, out-topping all. The forming of this figure in all
individuals, out of all materials, is the formation of a "cul-
ture." But when all figures are shattered, when no figure is
able any more to dominate and shape the present human material, what is there left to form?

Nothing but the image of God.

That is the indefinable, only factual, direction of the
responsible modern educator. This cannot be a theoretical
answer to the question "To what?," but only, if at all, an
answer carried out in deeds; a deed done by non-doing.

When all "directions" fail there arises in the darkness over
the abyss the one true direction of man, toward the creative
spirit, toward the spirit of God brooding on the face of the
waters, the spirit of which we know not whence it comes
and whither it goes.

That is man's true autonomy which no longer betrays,
but responds.

Man, the creature, who forms and transforms the creation,
cannot create. But he, each man, can expose himself and
others to the creative spirit. And he can call upon the Creator to save and perfect His image.

Education

○

The education I mean is a guiding toward reality and realization. That man alone is qualified to teach who knows how to distinguish between appearance and reality, between seeming realization and genuine realization, who rejects appearance and chooses and grasps reality, no matter what world-view he chooses. This education educates the adherents of all world-views to genuineness and to truth. It educates each of them to take his world-view seriously: to start from the genuineness of its ground and to move toward the truth of its goal.

Contact

Contact is the basic word in education. It means that the teacher must relate himself to his students not as one brain to other brains—a well-developed brain to still undeveloped ones—but as one being to other beings; as a mature being to maturing ones. He must meet them unequivocally, on their own level: his guidance should emanate not from above to below, from his lectern to their desks, but from a genuine interrelatedness and exchange of experience—the experiences of a full life and those of lives still unfulfilled but no less significant. What is required is not merely a search for information from below and a handing down of information from above, nor a mere interchange of questions and answers, but a genuine dialogue into which the teacher must enter directly and unselfconsciously, though he must also guide and control it. This dialogue ought to be continued until in fact it culminates in a wordless being-with-one-another. It is this that I call the dialogical principle of education.

Socratic and Mosaic Man

Man as a creature is able to make spirit independent of physical life. His great danger is that he may tolerate and even sanction existence on two different levels: one up above and fervently adored, the habitation of the spirit; and one down below, the dwelling of urges and petty concerns, equipped with a fairly good conscience acquired in hours of meditation in the upper story.

The teachings do not rely on the hope that he who knows them will also observe them. Socratic man believes that all virtue is cognition, and that all that is needed to do what is right is to know what is right. This does not hold for Mosaic man who is informed with the profound experience that cognition is never enough, that the deepest part of him must be seized by the teachings, that for realization to take place his elemental totality must submit to the spirit as clay to the potter.

The Struggle

I do not consider the individual to be either the starting point or the goal of the human world. But I consider the human person to be the irremovable central place of the struggle between the world's movement away from God and its movement toward God. This struggle takes place today to an uncannily large extent in the realm of public life, of course not between group and group but within each group. Yet the decisive battles of this realm as well are fought in the depth, in the ground or the groundlessness, of the person.

This Beloved Thing

The loving man is one who grasps non-relatively each thing he grasps. He does not think of inserting the experienced thing into relations to other things; at the moment of experience nothing else exists, nothing save this beloved thing, filling out the world and indistinguishably coinciding with it. Where you with agile fingers draw out the qualities common to all things and distribute them in ready-made categories, the loving man's dream-powerful and primally-awake heart beholds the non-common. This, the unique, is the bestowing shape, the self of the thing, that cannot be detained within the pure circle of world comprehensibility. What you extract and combine is always only the passivity of things. But their activity, their effective reality, reveals itself only to the loving man who knows them. And thus he knows the world. In the features of the beloved, whose self he realizes, he discerns the enigmatic countenance of the universe.

Human Pursuits

True art is a loving art. To him who pursues such art there appears, when he experiences an existent thing, the secret shape of that thing which appeared to none before him. This he does not see only with his eyes, rather he feels its outlines with his limbs; a heart beats against his heart. Thus he learns the glory of things so that he expresses them and praises them and reveals their shape to others.

True science is a loving science. The man who pursues such science is confronted by the secret life of things which has confronted none before him; this life places itself in his hands, and he experiences it, and is filled with its happening to the rim of his existence. Then he interprets what he has experienced in simple and fruitful concepts, and celebrates the unique and incomparable that happened to him with reverent honesty.

True philosophy is a loving philosophy. To him who pursues such philosophy a secret meaning opens, when he experiences a thing of the world—the law of that thing that opened itself to none before him. This meaning comes not as an object but as something that shatters him and discloses to him his own meaning—the meaning of all the years of his life and all its destiny, the meaning of his sorrowful and exalted thinking. So he receives the law of the thing which he perceived with obedient and creative soul, and establishes it as a law of the world; in so doing he has not been presumptuous but worthy and faithful.

Every true deed is a loving deed. All true deeds arise from contact with a beloved thing and flow into the universe. Any true deed brings, out of lived unity, unity into the world. Unity is not a property of the world but its task. To form unity out of the world is our never-ending work.

Death

○

We know nothing about death, nothing beyond the one
fact that we shall "die"—but what is that, to die? We do not
know. We must therefore assume that death constitutes the
final limit of all that we are able to imagine. The desire to
extend our imagination into the beyond of dying, to antici-
pate psychically what death alone can reveal to us existentially, seems to me to be a lack of faith disguised as faith.
Genuine faith says: I know nothing about death, but I do
know that God is eternity; and I also know that He is my
God. Whether what we call time will abide with us beyond
our death becomes rather insignificant for us compared to
the knowledge that we are God's—who is not "immortal"
but eternal. Instead of imagining ourselves to be alive yet
dead, we will prepare ourselves for a true death, which is
perhaps the terminal boundary of time, but, if so, certainly
also the threshold of eternity.

Satan

The name Satan means in Hebrew the hinderer. That is the true designation for the anti-human in individuals and in the human race. Let us not allow this Satanic element in men to hinder us from realizing man! Let us redeem speech from its ban! Let us dare, despite all, to trust!

HUMAN SPEECH AND DIALOGUE ❍ V

Language and Address

○

A precommunicative stage of language is unthinkable. Man did not exist before having a fellow being, before he lived over against him, toward him, and that means before he had dealings with him. Language never existed before address; it could become monologue only after dialogue broke off or broke down. The early speaker was not surrounded by objects on which he imposed names, nor did adventures befall him that he caught with names: the world and destiny became language for him only in partnership. Even when in a solitude beyond the range of call the hearerless word pressed against his throat, this word was connected with the primal possibility, that of being heard.

Distance and Relation

○

The solitary category "man" is to be understood as a working together of distance and relation. Unlike all other living beings, man stands over against a world from which he has been set at a distance and, unlike all other living beings, he can again and again enter into relationship with it. This fundamental double stance nowhere manifests itself so comprehensively as in language. Man—he alone—speaks, for only he can address the other just as the other being standing at a distance over against him; but in addressing it, he enters into relationship. The coming-to-be of language also means a new function of distance. For even the earliest speaking does not, like a cry or a signal, have its end in itself; it sets the word outside itself in being, and the word continues, it has continuance. And this continuance wins its life ever anew in true relation, in the spokenness of the word. Genuine dialogue witnesses to it, and poetry witnesses to it. For the poem is spokenness, spokenness to the Thou, wherever this partner might be.

The Partner

In genuine dialogue the turning to the partner takes place in all truth, that is, it is a turning of the being. Every speaker "means" the partner or partners to whom he turns as this personal existence. To "mean" someone in this connection is at the same time to exercise that degree of making present which is possible to the speaker at that moment. The experiencing senses and the imagining of the real which completes the findings of the senses work together to make the other present as a whole and as a unique being, as the person that he is. But the speaker does not merely perceive the one who is present to him in this way; he receives him as his partner, and that means that he confirms this other being, so far as it is for him to confirm. The true turning of his person to the other includes this confirmation, this acceptance. Of course, such a confirmation does not mean approval; but no matter in what I am against the other, by accepting him as my partner in genuine dialogue I have affirmed him as a person.

Without Reserve

○

Where the dialogue is fulfilled in its being, between partners who have turned to one another in truth, who express themselves without reserve and are free of the desire for semblance, there is brought into being a memorable common fruitfulness which is to be found nowhere else. At such times, at each such time, the word arises in a substantial way between men who have been seized in their depths and opened out by the dynamic of an elemental togetherness. The interhuman opens out what otherwise remains unopened.

Three Elements

❍

The truth of the word that is genuinely spoken is in its highest forms—in poetry and incomparably still more so in that messagelike saying that descends out of the stillness over a disintegrating human world—indivisible unity. It is a manifestation without a concomitant diversity of aspects. In all its other forms, however, three different elements must be distinguished in it. It is, in the first place, faithful truth in relation to the reality which was once perceived and is now expressed, to which it opens wide the window of language in order that it may become directly perceptible to the hearer. It is, second, faithful truth in relation to the person addressed, whom the speaker means as such, no matter whether he bears a name or is anonymous, is familiar or alien. And to mean a man means nothing less than to stand by him and his insight with the elements of the soul that can be sent forth, with the "outer soul," even though at the same time one fundamentally remains and must remain with oneself. Third, it is the truth of the word that is genuinely spoken, faithful truth in relation to its speaker, that is, to his factual existence in all its hidden structure. The human truth of which I speak—the truth vouchsafed men—is no pneuma that pours itself out from above on a band of men now become superpersonal: it opens itself to one just in one's existence as a person. This concrete person, in the life-space allotted to him, answers with his faithfulness for the word that is spoken by him.

Sharing of Knowledge

○

The genuine We is to be recognized in its objective existence, through the fact that in whatever of its parts it is regarded, an essential relation between person and person, between I and Thou, is always evident as actually or potentially existing. For the word always arises only between an I and a Thou, and the element from which the We receives its life is speech, the communal speaking that begins in the midst of speaking to one another.

Speech in its ontological sense was at all times present wherever men regarded one another in the mutuality of I and Thou; wherever one showed the other something in the world in such a way that from then on he began really to perceive it; wherever one gave another a sign in such a way that he could recognize the designated situation as he had not been able to before; wherever one communicated to the other his own experience in such a way that it penetrated the other's circle of experience and supplemented it as from within, so that from now on his perceptions were set within a world as they had not been before. All this flowing ever again into a great stream of reciprocal sharing of knowledge—thus came to be and thus is the living We, the genuine We, which, where it fulfils itself, embraces the dead who once took part in colloquy and now take part in it through what they have handed down to posterity.

The Central Question

During the First World War it became clear to me that a process was going on which before then I had only surmised. This was the growing difficulty of genuine dialogue, and most especially of genuine dialogue between men of different kinds and convictions. Direct, frank dialogue is becoming ever more difficult and more rare; the abysses between man and man threaten ever more pitilessly to become unbridgeable. I began to understand at that time . . . that this is the central question for the fate of mankind. Since then I have continually pointed out that the future of man as man depends upon a rebirth of dialogue.

The "Narrow Ridge"

○

Since my own thoughts over the last things reached, in the
First World War, a decisive turning-point, I have occasion-
ally described my standpoint to my friends as the "narrow
ridge." I wanted by this to express that I did not rest on the
broad upland of a system that includes a series of sure statements about the absolute, but on a narrow rocky ridge between the gulfs where there is no sureness of expressible
knowledge but the certainty of meeting with the One who
remains undisclosed.

Unity of Contraries

○

It is only when reality is turned into logic and A and non-A dare no longer dwell together, that we get determinism and indeterminism, a doctrine of predestination and a doctrine of freedom, each excluding the other. According to the logical conception of truth only one of two contraries can be true, but in the reality of life as one lives it they are inseparable. The person who makes a decision knows that his deciding is no self-delusion; the person who has acted knows that he was and is in the hand of God. The unity of the contraries is the mystery at the innermost core of the dialogue.

Acceptance of Otherness

Genuine conversation, and therefore every actual fulfilment of relation between men, means acceptance of otherness. When two men inform one another of their basically different views about an object, each aiming to convince the other of the rightness of his own way of looking at the matter, everything depends so far as human life is concerned on whether each thinks of the other as the one he is, whether each, that is, with all his desire to influence the other, nevertheless unreservedly accepts and confirms him in his being this man and in his being made in this particular way. The strictness and depth of human individuation, the elemental otherness of the other, is then not merely noted as the necessary starting point, but is affirmed from the one being to the other. The desire to influence the other then does not mean the effort to change the other, to inject one's own "rightness" into him; but it means the effort to let that which is recognized as right, as just, as true (and for that very reason must also be established there, in the substance of the other) through one's influence take seed and grow in the form suited to individuation. Opposed to this effort is the lust to make use of men by which the manipulator of "propaganda" and "suggestion" is possessed, in his relation to men remaining as in a relation to things, to things, moreover, with which he will never enter into relation, which he is indeed eager to rob of their distance and independence.

This Beloved Thing

○

Hallowing

The world is a creation, not a reflection, not semblance, not play. The world is not something which must be overcome. It is created reality, but reality created to be hallowed. Everything created has a need to be hallowed and is capable of receiving it: all created corporeality, all created urges and elemental forces of the body. Hallowing enables the body to fulfil the meaning for which it was created. The meaning with which creation informed men, informed the world, is fulfilled through the hallowing. Here, then, the world is neither transfigured into something wholly spiritual nor overcome by the spirit. The spirit does not embrace a holy world, rejoicing in its holiness, nor does it float above an unholy world, clutching all holiness to itself: it produces holiness, and the world is made holy.

Purpose

ᴑ

There is a purpose to creation; there is a purpose to the human race, one we have not made up ourselves, or agreed to among ourselves; we have not decided that henceforward this, that, or the other shall serve as the purpose of our existence. No. The purpose itself revealed its face to us and we have gazed upon it.

Grace

We are referred to grace; but we do not do God's will when we dare to begin with grace instead of beginning with ourselves. Only our beginning, our having begun, poor as it is, leads us toward grace. God made no tools for Himself, He needs none; He created for Himself a partner in a dialogue of time, one who is capable of holding dialogue. In this dialogue God speaks to every man through the life which He gives him again and again. Therefore man can only answer God with the whole of life—with the way in which he lives this given life.

Fellow-Creatures

○

We are created along with one another and directed to a life with one another. Creatures are placed in my way so that I, their fellow-creature, by means of them and with them find the way to God. A God reached by their exclusion would not be the God of all lives in whom all life is fulfilled.

The Stamp of Truth

We know that there is a truth which is the seal of God, and we know that the task we have been entrusted with is to let this one truth set its stamp on all the various facets of our life. We cannot own this truth, for it belongs to God. We ourselves cannot use the seal, but we can be the divers wax which takes the seal. Every individual is wax of a different form and color, but all are potentially receptive to the stamp of truth, for all of us, created "in the image of God," are potentially able to become images of the divine.

Whence Evil?

What we call "evil" is not merely in man; it is in the world as the bad; it is the uncleanness of creation. But this uncleanness is not a nature, not an existent property of things. It is only its not standing firm, not finding direction, not deciding.

God has created a world and has called what was created very good—where then does the bad come from? God has created a world and has celebrated its completion—where then does the incomplete come from?

The gnosis of all ages opposes to the good power of God another primal power that works evil; it wishes history to be viewed as the battle between these two powers and the redemption of the world as the victorious consummation of this battle. But we know what has been proclaimed by the anonymous prophet whose words stand in the second part of the Book of Isaiah: that like light and darkness, so good and evil have been created by God Himself. No uncreated power stands in opposition to Him.

Then is not the evil, the bad, a nature, an existent property after all? But the darkness also is no nature, but the abyss of the absence of light and the struggle for light and even as such created by God.

With All of One's Soul

With all of one's soul. He who decides with all of his soul decides for God; for all wholeness is God's image, shining from within with His own light. In that genuine, unifying decision in which dualism is abolished, the primeval intent of the world is fulfilled, in eternal renewal. . . .

The man confronted with decision sees his own duality as one of good and evil, that is, of a sense of direction and powerful impulses. Only a soul incapable of assembling its forces into a whole chooses evil: it lets its direction-less impulses take over. In the soul whose decision stems from its unity, impulse and sense of direction—the undiminished force of passionate drives and the unswerving directness of intent—are one. In the realm entrusted to him, such a man perfects the work of creation. And the perfection of any matter, the highest or lowest, touches on the divine.

Meet the World

○

Existence will remain meaningless for you if you yourself do not penetrate into it with active love and if you do not in this way discover its meaning for yourself. Everything is waiting to be hallowed by you; it is waiting to be disclosed in its meaning and to be realized in it by you. For the sake of this your beginning, God created the world. He has drawn it out of Himself so that you may bring it closer to Him. Meet the world with the fulness of your being and you shall meet Him. That He Himself accepts from your hands what you have to give to the world, is His mercy. If you wish to believe, love!

He who loves brings God and the world together.

The Basis

ɔ

The perception of revelation is the basis for perceiving creation and redemption. I begin to realize that in inquiring about my own origin and goal I am inquiring about something other than myself, and something other than the world. But in this very realization I begin to recognize the origin and goal of the world.

From Without

○

In revelation, something happens to man from out of a sphere that is neither man, nor soul, nor world. Revelation does not take place within man, nor can it be explained by a psychologism. Whoever talks of "the God within me" stands at the outermost periphery of being: there one cannot, must not, live. Revelation does not flow from the unconscious; it is master of the unconscious. Revelation comes as a power from without, but not in such a way as to make of man a vessel to be filled or a mere mouthpiece. Rather, it takes possession of the existent human element and recasts it: revelation is encounter's pure form.

Authentication

○

Every ethos has its origin in a revelation, whether or not it is still aware of and obedient to it; and every revelation is revelation of human service to the goal of creation, in which service man authenticates himself. Without authentication, that is, without setting off upon and keeping to the One direction, as far as he is able, *quantum satis*, man certainly has what he calls life, even the life of the soul, even the life of the spirit, in all freedom and fruitfulness, all standing and status —true being there is none for him without it.

Commandment

○

There is no revelation without commandment. Even when He who addresses us talks to us about Himself, he is really talking about us. What He says of Himself does not refer to His own being, but gives the reasons for and the elucidation of His demands on us. In that He addresses us, He distinguishes within human life between what is proper and what is not proper for man. Without ceasing to be the Absolute, that is, a power which cannot be identified with any attribute accessible to human understanding, He distinguishes between truth and lie, righteousness and unrighteousness. He challenges us to make such distinctions within the sphere of our life, just as He, in the sphere of nature, distinguished between the light and darkness He created. Our own life is, therefore, the only sphere in which we can point Him out, and then only through this life of ours.

God and the Neighbor

Both are to be "loved," God and the "neighbor" (that is, not man in general, but the man who meets me time and again in the context of life), but in different ways. The neighbor is to be loved "as one like myself" (not "as I love myself"; in the last reality one does not love oneself, but one should rather learn to love oneself through love of one's neighbor), to whom, then, I should show love as I wish it may be shown to me. But God is to be loved with all my soul and all my might. By connecting the two Jesus brings to light the Old Testament truth that God and man are not rivals. Exclusive love to God ("with all your heart") is, because he is God, inclusive love, ready to accept and include all love. It is not Himself that God creates, not Himself He redeems, even when He "reveals Himself" it is not Himself He reveals: His revelation does not have Himself as object. He limits Himself in all His limitlessness, He makes room for the creatures, and so, in love to Him, He makes room for love to the creatures.

Reason and Revelation

○

Revelation is unending, and anything is apt to become its sign. What is disclosed to us through revelation is not God's essence, independent of our existence, but His relation to us and our relation to Him. We are receptive to revelation only if, and as long as, we are a whole. This wholeness, which encompasses all our capacities and all our faculties, should not, of course, be devoid of reason. It, too, must become an integral part of that oneness which alone enables us to be receptive to revelation. But to do that it must relinquish its claim to self-sufficiency. Once reason has become one of the elements constituting the totality of our substance, it can no longer come to pass that whatever is experienced in revelation is contrary to reason itself; though it may well happen that it is contrary to the insights reason has gained so far. Having become an integral part of the whole, reason is willing to let its previous ascertainments be reversed, or at least corrected, by revelation. Hence revelation asks reason not only to participate in its reception, but also to let itself be stimulated by it, and renewed.

The Touch of the Other

○

Sometimes we have a personal experience related to those recorded as revelations and capable of opening the way for them. We may unexpectedly grow aware of a certain apperception within ourselves, which was lacking but a moment ago, and whose origin we are unable to discover. The attempt to derive such apperception from the famous unconscious stems from the widespread superstition that the soul can do everything by itself, and it fundamentally means nothing but this: what you have just experienced always was in you. Such notions build up a temporary construction which is useful for psychological orientation, but collapses when I try to stand upon it. But what occurred to me was "otherness," was the touch of the other. Nietzsche says it more honestly, "You take, you do not ask who it is that gives." But I think that as we take, it is of the utmost importance to know that someone is giving. He who takes what is given him, and does not experience it as a gift, is not really receiving; and so the gift turns into theft. But when we do experience the giving, we find out that revelation exists. And we set foot on the path which will reveal our life and the life of the world as a sign communication. This path is the approach.

Beginning and End

○

The man of today knows of no beginning. As far as he is concerned, history ripples toward him from some prehistorical cosmic age. He knows of no end; history sweeps him on into a posthistorical cosmic age. What a violent and foolish episode this time between the prehistorical and the posthistorical has become! Man no longer recognizes an origin or a goal because he no longer wants to recognize the midpoint. Creation and redemption are true only on the premise that revelation is a present experience. Man of today resists the Scriptures because he cannot endure revelation. To endure revelation is to endure this moment full of possible decisions, to respond to and to be responsible for every moment. Man of today resists the Scriptures because he does not want any longer to accept responsibility. He thinks he is venturing a great deal, yet he industriously evades the one real venture, that of responsibility.

Body, Soul, and Spirit

○

Just as God's cry of creation does not call to the soul, but to the wholeness of things, as revelation does not empower and require the soul, but all of the human being—so it is not the soul, but the whole of the world, which is meant to be redeemed in the redemption. Man stands created, a whole body, ensouled by his relation to the created, enspirited by his relation to the Creator. It is to the whole man, in this unity of body, soul, and spirit, that the Lord of Revelation comes and upon whom He lays His message. So it is not only with his thought and his feelings, but with the sole of his foot and the tip of his finger as well, that he may receive the sign-language of the reality taking place. The redemption must take place in the whole corporeal life. God the Creator wills to consummate nothing less than the whole of His creation; God the Revealer wills to actualize nothing less than the whole of His revelation; God the Redeemer wills to draw into His arms nothing less than the all in need of redemption.

Between Creation and Redemption

The lived moment of man stands in truth between creation
and redemption; it is joined to his being acted upon in creation, but also to his power to work for redemption. Rather,
he does not stand between the two but in both at once; for
as creation does not merely take place once in the beginning
but also at every moment throughout the whole of time, so
redemption does not take place merely once at the end but
also at every moment throughout the whole of time. The
moment is not merely joined to both, both are included in
it. Creation did not "really" take place once for all, nor is it
now merely "carried on," as it were, so that all acts of creation, including this one that now takes place, add up to the
work of creation. Rather, the word of the [Hebrew] prayer
book, that God renews the work of creation every day, is
entirely true. The act of creation that now takes place is
thus wholly capable of "beginning," and the creative moment
of God stands not only in the sequence of time, but in His
own absoluteness. As in the realm of creation, in which God
alone rules, the moment is thus not merely from somewhere,
but occurs out of itself and in itself, so is it in the realm of
redemption, in which God grants and demands that His
action should incomprehensibly enclose the action of the
human person.

Messianic Action

All mankind is accorded the co-working power, all time is directly redemptive, all action for the sake of God may be messianic action. But only unpremeditated action can be action for the sake of God. The self-differentiation, the reflection of man to a messianic superiority of this person, of this hour, of this action, destroys the unpremeditated quality of the act. Turning the whole of his life in the world to God and then allowing it to open and unfold in all its moments until the last—that is man's work toward redemption.

We live in an unredeemed world. But out of each human life that is unarbitrary and bound to the world, a seed of redemption falls into the world, and the harvest is God's.

The Moment

○

What approaches us cannot be known beforehand; God and the moment cannot be known beforehand; and the moment is God's moment; therefore, we can, indeed, prepare ourselves ever again for the deed, but we cannot prepare the deed itself. The substance of the deed is ever again given to us; rather, it is offered us: through that which happens to us, which meets us—through everything which meets us. Everything wants to be hallowed, to be brought into the holy, everything worldly in its worldliness: it does not want to be stripped of its worldliness, it wants to be brought in its worldliness into the true intent of redemption. . . . The creature seeks us, the things seek us out on our paths; what comes to meet us on our way needs us for its way. Everything wants to come to us, everything wants to come to God through us.

Jews and Christians

ᴑ

What have we and you in common? If we take the question literally, a book and an expectation.

To you the book is a forecourt; to us it is the sanctuary. But in this place we can dwell together, and together listen to the voice that speaks here. That means that we can work together to evoke the buried speech of that voice; together we can redeem the imprisoned living word.

Your expectation is directed toward a second coming, ours to a coming which has not been anticipated by a first. To you the phrasing of world history is determined by one absolute mid-point, the year zero; to us it is an unbroken flow of tones following each other without a pause from their origin to their consummation. But we can wait for the advent of the One together, and there are moments when we may prepare the way for Him together.

Pre-messianically our destinies are divided. Now to the Christian the Jew is the incomprehensibly obdurate man, who declines to see what has happened; and to the Jew the Christian is the incomprehensibly daring man, who affirms in an unredeemed world that its redemption has been accomplished. This is a gulf which no human power can bridge. But it does not prevent the common watch for a unity to come to us from God which, soaring above all of your imagination and all of ours, affirms and denies, denies and affirms what you hold and what we hold, and which replaces all the creedal truths of earth by the existential truth of heaven which is one.

All the Spheres of Man

○

We can only work on the kingdom of God through working on all the spheres of man that are allotted to us. There is
no universally valid choice of means to serve the purpose.
One cannot say, we must work here and not there, this leads
to the goal and that does not. . . . There is no legitimately
messianic, no legitimately messianically-intended, politics.
But that does not imply that the political sphere may be ex-
cluded from the hallowing of all things. The "serpent" is
not essentially evil, it is itself only misled; it, too, ultimately
wants to be redeemed. It does not avail to strike at it, it does
not avail to turn away from it. It belongs with the creaturely
world: we must have to do with it, without inflexible prin-
ciples, in naked responsibility.

God Waits for Man

◑

God wills to need man for the work of completing His creation; in this sentence is to be grasped the foundation of the Jewish doctrine of redemption. But that God wills this means that this "needing" becomes working reality: in history as it takes place, God waits for man.

COMMUNITY AND HISTORY ☉ VII

Life in Common

In the interests of its vital meaning the idea of community must be guarded against all contamination by sentimentality or emotionalism. Community is never a mere attitude of mind, and if it is feeling it is that of an inner constitution. . . . It is community of tribulation and, only because of that, community of spirit; community of toil and, only because of that, community of salvation. Even those communities which call the spirit their master and salvation their promised land, the "religious" communities, are community only if they serve their lord and master in the midst of simple, unexalted, unselected reality, a reality not so much chosen by them as sent to them just as it is; they are community only if they prepare the way to the promised land through the thickets of this pathless hour. True, it is not "works" that count, but the work of faith does. A community of faith truly exists only when it is a community of work.

Center

o

The real essence of community is to be found in the fact—
manifest or otherwise—that it has a center. The real beginning of a community is when its members have a common
relation to the center overriding all other relations: the circle
is described by the radii, not by the points along its circum-
ference. And the originality of the center cannot be discerned unless it is discerned as being transpicuous to the light
of something divine. All this is true; but the more earthly,
the more creaturely, the more attached the center is, the
truer and more transpicuous it will be. This is where the
"social" element comes in. Not as something separate, but as
the all-pervading realm where man stands the test; and it is
here that the truth of the center is proved.

The *Polis* of God

○

Certainly, when a religious man, one who is serious about his religiousness in any situation whatever, functions in the political sphere, religion is introduced into politics. But the way to the religious goal is essentially dissimilar in its conduct of affairs, its perspective, its manner of going, its tempo, and, lastly, in the unforeseeableness, if compared with political conduct. The holy cause of introducing the religious reality into politics runs the danger, therefore, that the categories will mingle, that the goal will become an end, the way a means; that man, instead of treading in the path taken by that step of God through history, will run blindly over it. If religion is threatened at one pole by the ice of isolation in which it forfeits a tie with the communal-building human share in the coming of the kingdom, here it is threatened by evaporation in the rapid fire of political activity. Only in the great *polis* of God will religion and politics be blended into a life of world community, in an eternity wherein neither religion nor politics will any longer exist.

Religious Socialism

Religious socialism cannot mean the joining of religion and socialism in such a manner that each of the constituents could achieve, apart from the other, independence if not fulfilment; it cannot mean merely that the two have concluded an agreement to unite their autonomies in a common being and working. Religious socialism can only mean that religion and socialism are essentially directed to each other, that each of them needs the covenant with the other for the fulfilment of its own mission. *Religio*, that is the human person's binding of himself to God, can only attain its full reality in the will for a community of the human race, out of which alone God can prepare His kingdom. *Socialitas*, that is mankind's becoming a fellowship, man's becoming a fellow to man, cannot develop otherwise than out of a common relation to the divine center, even if this be again and still nameless. Unity with God and community among the creatures belong together. Religion without socialism is disembodied spirit, therefore not genuine spirit; socialism without religion is body emptied of spirit, hence also not genuine body. But—socialism without religion does not hear the divine address, it does not aim at a response, yet still it happens that it responds; religion without socialism hears the call but does not respond.

Religion and Socialism

The point where religion and socialism can meet each other in the truth is the concrete personal life. As the truth of religion consists not of dogma or prescribed ritual but means standing and withstanding in the abyss of the real reciprocal relation with the mystery of God, so socialism in its truth is not doctrine and tactics but standing and withstanding in the abyss of the real reciprocal relation with the mystery of man. As it is presumption to believe in something without—however inadequately—living that in which one believes, so it is presumption to wish to accomplish something without —however inadequately—living what one wants to accomplish. As the "there" refuses to give itself to us when the "here" is not devoted to it, so the "then" must refuse when the "now" does not authenticate it. Religion must know that it is the everyday that sanctifies or desecrates devotion. And socialism must know that the decision as to how similar or dissimilar the end which is attained will be to the end which was previously cherished is dependent upon how similar or dissimilar to the set goal are the means whereby it is pursued. Religious socialism means that man in the concreteness of his personal life takes seriously the fundamentals of this life: the fact that God is, that the world is, and that he, this human person, stands before God and in the world.

Socialism

Socialism can never be anything absolute. It is the continual becoming of human community in mankind, adapted and proportioned to whatever can be willed and done in the conditions given. Rigidity threatens all realization, what lives and glows today may be crusted over tomorrow and, become all-powerful, suppress the strivings of the day after.

Pseudo-Realization

○

There can be pseudo-realization of socialism, where the real life of man to man is but little changed. The real living together of man with man can only thrive where people have the real things of their common life in common; where they can experience, discuss, and administer them together; where real fellowships and real work guilds exist. We see more or less from the Russian attempt at realization that human relationships remain essentially unchanged when they are geared to a socialist-centralist hegemony which rules the life of individuals and the life of the natural social groups. Needless to say we cannot and do not want to go back to primitive agrarian communism or to the corporate State of the Christian Middle Ages. We must be quite unromantic and, living wholly in the present, out of the recalcitrant material of our own day in history fashion a true community.

Three Covenants

Realization—that is the mystery of the covenant between God and man, presented in the threefold tale of the Scriptures: the first covenant with the lump of clay which the Creator, kneading, and by the breath of His mouth, imbues with His own likeness so that it might unfold in man's life and thus reveal that not being but becoming is man's task; the second covenant with the chosen patriarch, the covenant that begins with the parting from home and kin and is concluded with the demand for the sacrifice of the son, so that it might be revealed that realization requires the ultimate stake and unconditional surrender; the third covenant, in the Sinai desert, with the people whose first command is (Exodus 19:5 ff.) "You shall be for me a priestly realm, a holy people," so that it might be revealed that realization of the divine on earth is fulfilled not within man but between man and man, and that, though it does indeed have its beginning in the life of individual man, it is consummated only in the life of true community.

State

○

As to the problem of action Lenin starts off with a purely dialectical formula: "So long as there is a State there is no freedom. Once there is freedom there will be no more State." Such dialectics obscures the essential task which is to test day by day what the maximum of freedom is that can and may be realized today; to test how much "State" is still necessary today, and always to draw the practical conclusions. In all probability there will never—so long as man is what he is—be "freedom" pure and simple, and there will be "State," that is, compulsion, for just so long; the important thing, however, is the day to day question: no more State than is indispensable, no less freedom than is allowable. And freedom, socially speaking, means above all freedom for community, a community free and independent of State compulsion.

Meaning of History

If history is a dialogue between Deity and mankind, we can understand its meaning only when we are the ones who are addressed, and only to the degree to which we render ourselves receptive. We are, then, simply denied the capacity to judge current history and arrive at the conclusion that "This or that is its true meaning," or "This is what God intends, and that is contrary to God's will." But what we are permitted to know of history comes to this: "This, in one way or another, is history's challenge to me; this is its claim on me; and so this is its meaning as far as I am concerned."

This meaning, however, is not "subjective" in the sense that it originates in my emotion or cerebration, and then is transferred to objective happenings. Rather, it is the meaning I perceive, experience, and hear in reality. The meaning of history is not an idea that I can formulate independent of my personal life. It is only with my personal life that I am able to catch the meaning of history, for it is a dialogical meaning.

Goals

I should like to bring a concept of the utmost importance home even to those who cannot or will not understand the language of religion and, therefore, believe that I am discussing theology. I am speaking of the reality of history. In historical reality we do not set ourselves a just goal, choose whatever way to it an auspicious hour offers and, following that way, reach the set goal. If the goal to be reached is like the goal which was set, then the nature of the way must be like the goal. A wrong way, that is, a way in contradiction to the goal, must lead to a wrong goal. What is accomplished through lies, can assume the mask of truth; what is accomplished through violence, can go in the guise of justice, and for a while the hoax may be successful. But soon people will realize that lies are lies at bottom, that in the final analysis, violence is violence, and both lies and violence will suffer the destiny history has in store for all that is false. . . .

History has much to teach us, but we must know how to receive her teaching. These temporary successes which are apt to catch our attention are nothing but the stage-setting for universal history. If we keep our eyes fixed on the foreground, the true victories, won in secret, sometimes look like defeats. True victories happen slowly and imperceptibly, but they have far-reaching effects. In the limelight, our faith that God is the Lord of history may sometimes appear ludicrous; but there is an element in history which confirms our faith.

Freedom

○

Freedom—I love its flashing face: it flashes forth from the darkness and dies away, but it has made the heart invulnerable. I am devoted to it, I am always ready to join in the fight for it: for the sake of the appearance of the flash, which lasts no longer than the eye is able to endure it. I give my left hand to the rebel and my right to the heretic: forward! But I do not trust them. They know how to die, but that is not enough. I love freedom, but I do not believe in it.

The Revolutionary

The revolutionary lives on the knife's edge. The question that harasses him is, in fact, not merely the moral or religious one of whether he may kill; his quandary has nothing at all to do, as has at times been said, with "selling his soul to the devil" in order to bring the revolution to victory. His entanglement in the situation is here just the tension between end and means. I cannot conceive anything real corresponding to the saying that the end sanctifies the means; but I mean something which is real in the highest sense of the term when I say that the means profane, actually make meaningless, the end, that is, its realization! What is realized is the farther from the goal that was set, the more out of accord with it is the method by which it was realized. The ensuring of the revolution may only drain its heart's blood. The responsibility which results from these presuppositions must penetrate most deeply in the leader who is summoned to make the watchword of the spirit into the watchword of the event. But none of those who are led can neglect responsibility save by flight from self-recollection, that is, by the atrophy of the spirit within. The true front runs through the center.

Power

A great historian has asserted that power is evil. But this is not so. Power is intrinsically guiltless; it is the precondition for the actions of man. The problematic element is the will to power, greedy to seize and establish power, and not the effect of a power whose development was internal. A will to power, less concerned with being powerful than with being "more powerful than," becomes destructive. Not power but power hysteria is evil.

Will to Power

○

To strive for power for power's sake means to strive for nothing. He who seizes empty power ultimately grasps at emptiness. Will to power because one needs power to realize the truth in which one believes has a constructive strength; will to power as power leads from the self-aggrandizement of the individuals to the self-destruction of the people.

Power without genuine responsibility is a dazzlingly clothed impotence. The stronger battalions that believe in nothing save the leader are the weaker battalions. Their powerlessness will become manifest in the hour when they must vie with a strength born of belief. Those who depend upon empty power will be dragged down in its collapse.

Religion and Politics

Religion means goal and way, politics implies end and means. The political end is recognizable by the fact that it may be attained—in success—and its attainment is historically recorded. The religious goal remains, even in man's highest experiences, that which simply provides direction on the mortal way; it never enters into historical consummation. The history of the created world, as the religions believing in history acknowledge it, and the history of the human person, as all religions, even those that do not believe in history, acknowledge it, is what takes place on the journey from origin to perfection, and this is registered by other signs than that of success. "The Word" is victorious, but otherwise than its bearers hoped for. The Word is not victorious in its purity, but in its corruption; it bears its fruit in the *corruptio seminis*. Here no success is experienced and recorded; where something of the kind appears in the history of religion, it is no longer religion that prevails, but politics of religion. . . .

Non-Action

○

I believe that we can receive in a living manner something of the Taoist teaching of non-action, the teaching of Lao-tzu. And for the reason that—bearing our burden on our way—we have learned something analogous, only negatively—on the reverse side, so to speak. We have begun to learn, namely, that success is of no consequence. We have begun to doubt the significance. of historical success, that is, the validity of the man who sets an end for himself, carries this end into effect, accumulates the necessary means of power, and succeeds with these means of power: the typical modern Western man. I say, we begin to doubt the content of existence of this man. And there we come into contact with something genuine and deeply Chinese, though not, to be sure, Confucian: with the teaching that genuine effecting is not interfering, not giving vent to power, but remaining within one's self. This is the powerful existence that does not yield historical success, that is, the success that can be exploited and registered in this hour, but only yields that effecting that at first appears insignificant, indeed invisible, yet endures across generations and there at times becomes perceptible in another form.

At the core of each historical success hides the turning away from what the man who accomplished it really had in mind. Not realization, but the hidden non-realization that has been disguised or masked just through success is the mark of true historical success.

Transformation

◯

Toward the end of the first third of that same century in which those apocalypses were produced that spoke of the aged world and announced the approaching rupture of history, John the Baptist had again taken up the cry of the prophets, "Return!"; and, in complete accord with their belief in real alternatives, he had joined to the imperative the warning that the axe had already been laid to the roots of the tree. He trusted his hearers to trust themselves as capable of the turning that was demanded, and he trusted the human world of his hour to be capable of just this turning, of risk, of giving oneself, of inner transformation. After Jesus and in like manner his emissaries had sounded the call afresh, the apocalyptics and their associates proceeded to disclose that there is no turning and no new direction in the destiny of the world that can issue from the turning. But the depths of history, which are continually at work to rejuvenate creation, are in league with the prophets.

History and Eternity

○

The existentialism of Heidegger is rooted in Hegel's thought, in the deepest possible level. For Hegel world history is the absolute process in which the spirit attains to consciousness of itself; so for Heidegger historical existence is the illumination of being itself; in neither is there room for a supra-historical reality that sees history and judges it. For both philosophers the historical allows itself to be sanctioned in the last resort by its own thought concerning history; here as there, accordingly, reflection on man's boldest concept, that of eternity set in judgment above the whole course of history and thereby above each historical age, is not admitted. Time is not embraced by the timeless, and the ages do not shudder before One who does not dwell in time but only appears in it. The knowledge has vanished that time can in no wise be conceived as a finally existing reality, independent and self-contained, and that absurdity lies in wait for every attempt to reflect on it in this way no matter whether time be contemplated as finite or as infinite. If historical time and history are made absolute, it can easily occur that in the midst of present historical events the time-bound thinker ascribes to the state's current drive to power the character of an absolute and in this sense the determination of the future. After that, the goblin called success, convulsively grinning, may occupy for a while the divine seat of authority.

War and Peace

○

Hearkening to the human voice, where it speaks forth un-falsified, and replying to it, this above all is needed today. The busy noise of the hour must no longer drown out the *vox humana*, the essence of the human which has become a voice. This voice must not only be listened to, it must be answered and led out of the lonely monologue into the awakening dialogue of the peoples. Peoples must engage in talk with one another through their truly human men if the great peace is to appear and the devastated life of the earth renew itself.

The great peace is something essentially different from the absence of war.

In an early mural in the town hall of Siena the civic virtues are assembled. Worthy, and conscious of their worth, the women sit there, except one in their midst who towers above the rest. This woman is marked not by dignity but rather by composed majesty. Three letters announce her name: Pax. She represents the great peace I have in mind. This peace does not signify that what men call war no longer exists now that it holds sway—that means too little to enable one to understand this serenity. Something new exists, now really exists, greater and mightier than war, greater and mightier even than war. Human passions flow into war as the waters into the sea, and war disposes of them as it likes. But these passions must enter into the great peace as ore into the fire that melts and transforms it. Peoples will then build with one another with more powerful zeal than they have ever destroyed one another.

The Covenant of Men

○

The West cannot and may not abandon modern civilization, the East will not be able to shun it. But just the work of mastering these materials, of humanizing this materiality, the hallowing of this world, our own world, will lead the two hemispheres together through establishing here and there the covenant of men faithful to the Great Reality. The flaming sword of the *cherubim* circling the entrance of Paradise prohibits the way back. But it illumines the way forward.

ISRAEL
JEWISH EXISTENCE ○ **VIII**

Life Itself

○

The great deed of Israel is not that it taught the one real God, who is the origin and goal of all being, but that it pointed out that this God can be addressed by man in reality, that man can say Thou to Him, that he can stand face to face with Him, that he can have intercourse with Him. Wherever there is man, to be sure, there is also prayer, and so it has probably always been. But only Israel has understood, or rather actually lives, life as being addressed and answering, addressing and receiving answer.

God in all concreteness as speaker, the creation as speech: God's call into nothing and the response of things through their coming into existence, the speech of creation enduring in the life of all creation, the life of each creature as dialogue, the world as word—to proclaim this Israel existed. It taught, it showed, that the real God is the God who can be addressed because He is the God who addresses.

Unity

It is the striving for unity that has made the Jew creative. Striving to evolve unity out of the division of his I, he conceived the idea of the unitary God. Striving to evolve unity out of the division of the human community, he conceived the idea of universal justice. Striving to evolve unity out of the division of all living matter, he conceived the idea of universal love. Striving to evolve unity out of the division of the world, he created the messianic ideal, which later, again under the participation of some Jews, was reduced in scope, made finite, and called socialism.

Teaching and Life

○

Among all the peoples in the world, Israel is probably the only one in which wisdom that does not lead directly to the unity of knowledge and deed is meaningless. This becomes most evident when we compare the Biblical concept of *hokhmah* with the Greek concept of *sophia*. The latter specifies a closed realm of thought, knowledge for its own sake. It is totally alien to the *hokhmah*, which regards such a delimitation of an independent spiritual sphere, governed by its own laws, as the misconstruction of meaning, the violation of continuity, the severance of thought from reality.

The supreme command of *hokhmah* is the unity of teaching and life, for only through this unity can we recognize and avow the all-embracing unity of God.

Presence

◐

True human life is conceived to be a life lived in the presence of God. For Judaism, God is not a Kantian idea but an elementally present spiritual reality—neither something conceived by pure reason nor something postulated by practical reason but emanating from the immediacy of existence as such, the mystery of immediacy which religious man steadfastly faces and nonreligious man evades. God is the sun of mankind. However, it is not the man who turns his back on the world of things, staring into the sun in self-oblivion, who will remain steadfast and live in the presence of God, but only that man who breathes, walks, and bathes his self and all things in the sun's light. He who turns his back on the world comprehends God solely as idea, and not as reality. . . .

In Heaven and on Earth

○

[In Judaism] God is wholly raised above man, He is beyond the grasp of man, and yet He is present in an immediate relationship with these human beings who are absolutely incommensurable with Him, and He faces them. To know both these things at the same time, so that they cannot be separated, constitutes the living core of every believing Jewish soul; to know both, "God in heaven," that is, in complete hiddenness, and man "on earth," that is, in the fragmentation of the world of his senses and his understanding; God in the perfection and incomprehensibility of His being, and man in the abysmal contradiction of this strange existence from birth to death—and between both, immediacy!

Memory

◔

We Jews are a community based on memory. A common memory has kept us together and enabled us to survive. This does not mean that we based our life on any one particular past, even on the loftiest of pasts; it simply means that one generation passed on to the next a memory which gained in scope—for new destiny and new emotional life were constantly accruing to it—and which realized itself in a way we can call organic. This expanding memory was more than a spiritual motif; it was a power which sustained, fed, and quickened Jewish existence itself. I might even say that these memories realized themselves biologically, for in their strength the Jewish substance was renewed.

The God of Sinai

If we were only one nation among others, we should long ago have perished from the earth. Paradoxically we exist only because we dared to be serious about the unity of God and His undivided, absolute sovereignty. If we give up God, He will give us up. And we do give Him up when we profess Him in synagogue and deny Him when we come together for discussion, when we do His commands in our personal life, and set up other norms for the life of the group we belong to. What is wrong for the individual cannot be right for the community; for if it were, then God, the God of Sinai, would no longer be the Lord of peoples, but only of individuals. If we really are Jews, we believe that God gives His commands to men to observe throughout their whole life, and that whether or not life has a meaning depends on the fulfilment of those commands.

The King

○

In order to be lived, Jewish religiosity needs this people whose very peoplehood is to be constituted by its faith. Faith alone, and revelation, created this peoplehood: only through receiving the Word did this people come into being; and its legitimate existence was contingent on the condition that it would be ready to consummate this faith in the totality of life. Nor was it given a faith that claims only part of man, a faith merely hovering over the waters. The essential fact, on the contrary, is that faith cannot be content with just one compartment of life; rather, ever since its beginnings at Sinai, it has insisted on claiming all of life, as indeed it must. This total claim was made, and acknowledged, when the multitude assembled at the foot of the mountain pronounced, in communion, the Word of God. The faith becomes manifest in the fact that this multitude, having only now become a people, had already proclaimed the Lord of the Word as its only king before coming to the foot of the mountain. And king He remains, through time and eternity.

Prophetic Criticism

○

A people which seriously calls God Himself its king must become a true people, a community where all members are ruled by honesty without compulsion, kindness without hypocrisy, and the brotherliness of those who are passionately devoted to their divine leader. When social inequality, distinction between the free and the unfree, splits the community and creates chasms between its members, there can be no true people, there can be no "God's people." So [prophetic] criticism and demand are directed toward every individual whom other individuals depend upon, toward everyone who has a hand in shaping the destinies of others; that means directed toward every one of us. When Isaiah speaks of justice, he is not thinking of institutions but of you and me, because without you and me the most glorious institution becomes a lie.

The Ten Commandments

○

The Ten Commandments are not part of an impersonal codex governing an association of men. They were uttered by an I and addressed to a Thou. They begin with the I and every one of them addresses the Thou in person. An I "commands" and a Thou—every Thou who hears this Thou —"is commanded."

In the Decalogue, the Word of Him who issues commands is equipped with no executive power effective on the plane of predictable causality. The Word does not enforce its own hearing. Whoever does not wish to respond to the Thou addressed to him can apparently go about his business unimpeded. Though He who speaks the Word has power (and the Decalogue presupposes that He had sufficient power to create the heavens and the earth) He has renounced this power of His sufficiently to let every individual actually decide for himself whether he wants to open or close his ears to the voice, and that means whether he wants to choose or reject the I of "I am." He who rejects Him is not struck down by lightning; he who elects Him does not find hidden treasures. Everything seems to remain just as it was. Obviously, God does not wish to dispense either medals or prison sentences.

This, then, is the situation in which "faith" finds itself.

Covenant

☾

Israel is a people like no other, for it is the only one in the
world which, from its earliest beginnings, has been both a
nation and a religious community. In the historical hour in
which its tribes grew together to form a people, it became
the carrier of a revelation. The covenant which the tribes
made with one another and through which they became
"Israel" takes the form of a common covenant with the God
of Israel.

Biblical Leadership

The Biblical question of leadership is concerned with something greater than moral perfection. The Biblical leaders are the foreshadowings of the dialogical man, of the man who commits his whole being to God's dialogue with the world, and who stands firm throughout this dialogue. . . . Whatever the way, man enters into the dialogue again and again; imperfect entry, but yet one which is not refused, an entry which is determined to persevere in the dialogical world. All that happens is here experienced as dialogue, what befalls man is taken as a sign, what man tries to do and what miscarries is taken as an attempt and a failure to respond, as a stammering attempt to carry out responsibility as well as one can.

Success and Failure

○

The Bible knows nothing of an intrinsic value of success. On the contrary, when it announces a successful deed, it is duty-bound to announce in complete detail the failure involved in the success. When we consider the history of Moses we see how much failure is mingled in the one great successful action, so much so that when we set the individual events which make up his history side by side, we see that his life consists of one failure after another, through which runs the thread of his success. True, Moses brought the people out of Egypt; but each stage of this leadership is a failure. Whenever he comes to deal with this people, he is defeated by them, let God ever so often interfere and punish them. And the real history of this leadership is not the history of the exodus, but the history of the wandering in the desert. The personal history of Moses' own life, too, does not point back to his youth, and to what grew out of it; it points beyond, to death, to the death of the unsuccessful man, whose work, it is true, survives him, but only in new defeats, new disappointments, and continual new failures—and yet his work survives also in a hope beyond all these failures.

Prophetic Faith

The prophetic faith involves the faith in the factual character of human existence, as existence that factually meets transcendence. Prophecy has in its way declared that the unique being, man, is created to be a center of surprise in creation. Because and so long as man exists, factual change of direction can take place towards salvation as well as towards disaster, starting from the world in each hour, no matter how late. This message has been proclaimed by the prophets to all future generations, to each generation in its own language.

[This] view preserves the mystery of the dialogical intercourse between God and man from all desire for dogmatic encystment. The mystery is that of man's creation as a being with the power of actually choosing between the ways, who ever again and even now has the power to choose between them. Only such a being is suited to be God's partner in the dialogue of history. The future is not fixed, for God wants man to come to Him with full freedom, to return to Him even out of a plight of extreme hopelessness and then to be really with Him. This is the prophetic *theologem*, never expressed as such but firmly embedded in the foundations of Hebrew prophecy.

Prophecy and Apocalyptic

Prophecy and apocalyptic, regarded through their writings, are unique manifestations in the history of the human spirit and of its relationship to transcendence. Prophecy originates in the hour of the highest strength and fruitfulness of the Eastern spirit, the apocalyptic out of the decadence of its cultures and religions. But wherever a living historical dialogue of divine and human actions breaks through, there persists, visible or invisible, a bond with the prophecy of Israel. And wherever man shudders before the menace of his own work and longs to flee from the radically demanding historical hour, there he finds himself near to the apocalyptic vision of a process that cannot be arrested.

Community

○

The prophets knew and predicted that in spite of all its veer-
ing and compromising Israel must perish if it intends to exist
only as a political structure. It can persist—and this is the
paradox in their warning and the paradox of the reality of
Jewish history—if it insists on its vocation of uniqueness, if
it translates into reality the divine words spoken during the
making of the Covenant. When the prophets say that
there is no security for Israel save that in God, they are not
referring to something unearthly, to something "religious"
in the common sense of the word; they are referring to the
realization of the true communal living to which Israel was
summoned by the Covenant with God, and which it is
called upon to sustain in history, in the way it alone is capable of. The prophets call upon a people which represents
the first real attempt at "community" to enter world history
as a prototype of that attempt. Israel's function is to encour-
age the nations to change their inner structure and their relations to one another. By maintaining such relations with
the nations and being involved in the development of humanity, Israel may attain its unimperiled existence, its true
security.

The Message of Hasidism

○

Preserving both its epic and its mythical elements, I have
tried to bring to modern Western man the Hasidic teaching of life. It has often been suggested to me that I should
free this teaching from its "confessional limitation," as people are fond of putting it, and proclaim it as an unfettered
doctrine for humanity. But to enter such a "universal" path
would be for me pure wilfulness. In order to speak to the
world of what I have received I am not bound to step forth
into the street; I can remain within the doorway of my an-
cestral home. Even the word that is uttered there does not
get lost.

Hasidic teaching says that the worlds could fulfil their
destiny of becoming one by virtue of the life of man becoming one. But how is that to be understood? Is not a complete unity of living being inconceivable except in God
Himself? Israel's acknowledgment of the unity of God does
not merely state that there is no God beside Him but also
that He alone is unity. Here the interpreter must come to
our aid. If man can become "humanly" holy, that is, as a
man and to the degree and in the way of a man; and if, as
is written, he can become holy "unto me," that is, in the
sight of God, then he, the individual man, can become one
in the sight of God to the extent of his personal ability. Man
cannot approach the divine by going beyond the human.
But he can approach it by becoming the man that he, this
individual man, was created to become. This seems to me
the eternal essence of Hasidic life and Hasidic teaching.

To Gandhi

○

You say it is a stigma against us that our ancestors crucified Jesus. I do not know whether that actually happened, but I consider it possible. I consider it just as possible as that the Indian people under different circumstances should condemn you to death. . . . Not infrequently nations swallow up the greatness to which they have given birth. How can one assert, without contradiction, that such action constitutes a stigma! I would not deny, however, that although I should not have been among the crucifiers of Jesus, I should also not have been among his supporters. For I cannot help withstanding evil when I see that it is about to destroy the good. I am forced to withstand the evil in the world just as the evil within myself. I can only strive not to have to do so by force. I do not want force. But if there is no other way of preventing the evil destroying the good, I trust I shall use force and give myself up into God's hands. . . . If I am to confess what is truth to me, I must say: There is nothing better for a man than to deal justly—unless it be to love; we should be able even to fight for justice—but to fight lovingly.

On Accepting a German Award

The preparation for the final battle of *homo humanus* against *homo contrahumanus* has begun in the depths. But the front is split into as many individual fronts as there are peoples, and those who stand on one of the individual fronts know little or nothing of the other fronts. Darkness still covers the struggle, upon whose course and outcome it depends whether, despite all, a true humanity can issue from the race of men. The so-called cold war between two gigantic groups of states with all its accompaniments still obscures the true obligation and solidarity of combat, whose line cuts right through all states and peoples, however they name their régimes. The recognition of the deeper reality, of the true need and the true danger, is growing. In Germany, and especially in German youth, despite their being rent asunder, I have found more awareness of it than elsewhere. The memory of the twelve-year reign of *homo contrahumanus* has made the spirit stronger, and the task set by the spirit clearer, than they formerly were.

Tokens such as the bestowal of the Hanseatic Goethe Prize and the Peace Prize of the German Book Trade on a surviving arch-Jew must be understood in this connection. They, too, are moments in the struggle of the human spirit against the demonry of the subhuman and the antihuman. The survivor who is the object of such honors is taken up into the high duty of solidarity that extends across the fronts: the solidarity of all separate groups in the flaming battle for the rise of a true humanity. This duty is, in the present hour, the highest duty on earth. The Jew chosen as symbol must obey this call of duty even there, indeed, precisely there where the never-to-be-effaced memory of what has happened stands in opposition to it. When he recently expressed his gratitude to the spirit of Goethe, victoriously disseminated throughout the world, and when he now expresses his gratitude to the spirit of peace, which now as so often before speaks to the world in books of the German tongue, his thanks signify his confession of solidarity with the common battle—common also to Germans and Jews —against the contrahuman, and his reply to a vow taken by fighters, a vow he has heard.

Peace

◐

We make peace, we help bring about world peace, if we make peace wherever we are destined and summoned to do so: in the active life of one's own community and in that aspect of it which can actively help determine its relationship to another community. The prophecy of peace addressed to Israel is not valid only for the days of the coming of the Messiah. . . . Fulfilment in a "then" is inextricably bound up with fulfilment in the "now."

Another World?

Israel's faith in the redemption of the world does not mean that this world is to be redeemed by another one; it is, rather, a faith in a new world on this earth. The words "trans-mundane" and "mundane" do not exist in the Hebrew language. This hope, which encompasses the whole world, means that we cannot talk with God if we leave the world to its own devices. We can talk with God only by embracing the world, to the best of our ability; that is, by infusing everything with God's truth and justice.

The Kingdom of God

○

There is no re-establishing of Israel, there is no security for it save one: it must assume the burden of its own uniqueness; it must assume the yoke of the kingdom of God.

EPILOGUE ❦ Renewal

Renewal of Relation

○

All great civilization has been in a certain measure a civilization of the dialogue. The life substance of them all was not,
as one customarily thinks, the presence of significant individuals, but their genuine intercourse with one another. Individuation was only the presupposition for the unfolding
of dialogical life. What one calls the creative spirit of men
has never been anything other than the address, the cogita-
tive or artistic address, of those called to speak to those really
able and prepared to hear. . . .

There interposed in all times, of course, severe checks and
disturbances; there was closedness and unapproachableness,
dissembling and seduction. But where the human wonder
bloomed time and again, these checks and disturbances were
always overcome through the elemental power of men's
mutual confirmation. The one turned to the other as to a
unique personal being, undamaged by all error and trouble,
and received the other's turning to him. The one traced the
other in his being, in that in him which survived all illusions,
and even if they fought each other, they confirmed each
other as what they were. Man wishes to be confirmed by
man as he who he is, and there is genuine confirmation
only in mutuality.

Despite the progressive decline of dialogue and the corresponding growth of universal mistrust which characterize
our time, the need of men to be confirmed still continues.
But for the most part it no longer finds any natural satisfac-
tion. As a result, man sets out on one of two false ways: he
seeks to be confirmed either by himself or by a collective to
which he belongs. Both undertakings must fail. The self-
confirmation of him whom no fellow man confirms cannot
stand. With ever more convulsive exertions, he must en-

deavor to restore it, and finally he knows himself as inevitably abandoned. Confirmation through the collective, on the other hand, is pure fiction. It belongs to the nature of the collective, to be sure, that it accepts and employs each of its members as this particular individual, constituted and endowed in this particular way. But it cannot recognize anyone in his own being, and therefore independently of his usefulness for the collective. Modern man, insofar as he has surrendered direct and personal mutuality with his fellows, can only exchange an illusory confirmation for the one that is lost. There is no salvation save through the renewal of the dialogical relation, and this means, above all, through the overcoming of existential mistrust.

The Neighbor

○

Man's unacknowledged secret is his desire to be affirmed
in his essence and in his existence by his fellow men. He
wishes that they, in turn, would make it possible for him to
affirm them, and for both affirmations to be conferred not
merely within the family, or perhaps at a party meeting or
in a bar, but also in the course of neighborly encounters
when perhaps the greeting with which they hail each other
as they emerge from their houses or step to their windows
is accompanied by a kindly look, a look in which all curi-
osity, distrust, or the routine has been overcome by mutual
sympathy; by so doing, each would let the other know that
he endorses his presence. It is this endorsement that constitutes the indispensable minimum of man's humanity.

Confirmation

○

Man wishes to be confirmed in his being by man, and wishes to have a presence in the being of the other. The human person needs confirmation because man as man needs it. An animal does not need to be confirmed, for it is what it is unquestionably. It is different with man: sent forth from the natural domain of species into the hazard of the solitary category, surrounded by the air of a chaos which came into being with him, secretly and bashfully he watches for a Yes which allows him to be and which can come to him only from one human person to another.

Thanksgiving

○

The older we get, the greater becomes our inclination to give thanks, especially heavenwards. We feel more strongly than we could possibly have ever felt before that life is a free gift, and receive every unqualifiedly good hour in gratefully reaching out hands, as an unexpected gift.

But we also feel, again and again, an urge to thank our fellow man, even if he has not done anything special for us. For what, then? For really meeting me when we met; for opening his eyes, and not mistaking me for someone else; for opening his ears, and listening carefully to what I had to say to him; indeed, for opening up to me what I really wanted to address—his securely locked heart.

This is an hour of great thanksgiving. As I am writing this, I have before me, in a beautiful, enormous box made by my granddaughter, all the testimonials I have received on this day, which marks a milestone on the road of my life, from people whom I have met on the way, in body or in spirit; and stored in my memory, I keep all the direct testimonials.

The thanks I here express to all are not addressed to a mere aggregate of people; they are addressed to every single individual personally.

Acknowledgments

The editor gratefully acknowledges the permissions granted by the following publishers, translators, and editors to use their respective translations of Buber's writings:

Harper & Row, Publishers, Inc., for *Eclipse of God: Studies in the Relation between Religion and Philosophy*, translated by Maurice Friedman, Eugene Kamenka, and I. M. Lask, Copyright 1952 by Harper & Brothers; *The Knowledge of Man: Selected Essays*, edited by Maurice Friedman, translated by Maurice Friedman and Ronald Gregor Smith, Copyright © 1965 by Martin Buber and Maurice Friedman; *Pointing the Way: Collected Essays*, translated and edited by Maurice Friedman, Copyright © 1957 by Martin Buber.

Horizon Press, Publishers, for *The Origin and Meaning of Hasidism*, edited and translated by Maurice Friedman, Copyright 1960 by Martin Buber.

Horovitz Publishing Co., Ltd., for "Hasidism and Modern Man," *Between East and West:* Essays dedicated to the memory of Bela Horovitz, edited by A. Altmann, 1958.

The Macmillan Company, for *Between Man and Man*, translated by Ronald Gregor Smith, Copyright 1948 by Macmillan Company; *Paths in Utopia*, translated by R. F. C. Hull, Copyright 1949 by Martin Buber.

The Philosophical Library, Inc., for *Hasidism*, Copyright 1948 by The Philosophical Library, Inc.

Routledge & Kegan Paul Ltd., for *At the Turning*, Copyright 1952 by Martin Buber.

Schocken Books Inc., for *Israel and the World: Essays in a Time of Crisis*, translated by Greta Hort, Olga Marx, and I. M.

Exact references to the passages from the works here listed are to be found in the Bibliographical Guide. In that Guide the first mention of a book gives all details; the second and following mentions refer to the title only. "See" followed by a title refers to a title of a passage in the volume mentioned before in the Guide.

Bibliographical Guide

PROLOGUE: RESPONSE

A conversion: From *Die Kreatur* III, 3 (1929); *Zwiesprache*, Berlin, 1932, pp. 37-40; "Dialogue," *Between Man and Man*, London, 1947, pp. 13 f. Tr. Ronald Gregor Smith.

Response: From an address at the Third International Educational Conference in Heidelberg, Germany, August, 1925. *Rede über das Erzieherische*, Berlin, 1926. "Education," *Between Man and Man*, p. 92.

Responsibility: See "A conversion." *Between Man and Man*, p. 16.

Ethics: From a lecture prepared in 1928 for an institute of political science in Reichenhall, and later delivered at the *Weltwirtschaftliches Institut* in Kiel, Germany. *Volk und Reich der Deutschen*, ed. B. Harms, Berlin, 1929; "Der Glaube des Judentums," *Kampf um Israel*, Berlin, 1933, p. 37; "The Faith of Judaism," *Israel and the World*, New York, 1948, p. 19.

Reality: See "A conversion." *Between Man and Man*, p. 12.

I. GOD

Who speaks?: See "A conversion." *Between Man and Man*, pp. 14 f.

Absolute personality: Keneset . . . *le-zekher H. N. Bialik* VIII (1943); "The Love of God and the Idea of Deity," *Israel and the World*, New York, 1948, p. 63.

God and world: Be-fardes ha-hasidut, Tel Aviv, 1945; "Love of God and Love of One's Neighbor," *Hasidism*, New York, 1948, p. 170. Tr. I. Olsvanger and revised by Canon Witton-Davies.

Spirit and nature: From an address delivered in Stuttgart, Germany, March, 1930. *Der Morgen* VIII (1932); "Die Brennpunkte der jüdischen Seele," *Kampf um Israel*, p. 59; "The Two Foci of the Jewish Soul," *Israel and the World*, p. 34.

Wholeness alone: See "God and world." *Hasidism*, pp. 167 f.

Not what but how: From "Jüdische Religiosität," *Vom Geist des Judentums*, Leipzig, 1916; *Reden über das Judentum*, Berlin, 1932, pp. 112 f. *On Judaism*, pp. 86 f.

Symbols: From "Cheruth," an address, Vienna, 1919; *Reden über das Judentum*, pp. 202 f. *On Judaism*, pp. 150 f.

Transcendence: "Religion und Philosophie," *Sechzehntes Jahrbuch der Schopenhauer-Gesellschaft*, Heidelberg, 1929; "Religion and Philosophy," *Eclipse of God*, New York, 1952, p. 40. Tr. Maurice Friedman.

Dualism: From an address in Antwerp, Belgium, 1932. *Jüdische Rundschau*, Berlin, September 6, 1932; *Kampf um Israel*, pp. 454 f.; "And If Not Now, When?" *Israel and the World*, pp. 235 f.

Imitatio: See "Spirit and nature." *Israel and the World*, p. 32.

Unity: See "Spirit and nature." *Israel and the World*, p. 39.

The secret and the manifest: From "Nachahmung Gottes," *Der Morgen* I (1926); "Imitatio dei," *Kampf um Israel*, pp. 81 ff.; *Israel and the World*, pp. 76 f.

Images: From an address in Prague, 1937; *Worte an die Jugend*, Berlin, 1938, pp. 74-86. "Prejudices of Youth," *Israel and the World*, pp. 50 f.

The word and the name: Written in 1932. From "Report on Two Talks," *Eclipse of God*, pp. 17 f. Tr. Maurice Friedman.

God as a Person: I and Thou, p. 135.

Spinoza: From the introduction to *Die chassidischen Bücher*, Berlin, 1927. "Spinoza, Sabbatai Zvi, and the Baal-Shem," *The Origin and Meaning of Hasidism*, New York, 1960, pp. 92 f.

II. I AND THOU

Limits: From "Urdistanz und Beziehung," *Studia philosophica* X, Basel, 1950; "Distance and Relation," *Hibbert Journal*

XLIX (1951); *The Knowledge of Man,* New York, 1965, p. 69. Tr. Ronald Gregor Smith.

The primary word: From *Ich und Du,* Leipzig, 1923, p. 18; *I and Thou,* second edition, New York, 1958, p. 11.

Obstacles: Ich und Du, pp. 18 f.; *I and Thou,* pp. 11 f.

It-Thou: Ich und Du, pp. 43 and 114; *I and Thou,* pp. 34 and 98.

The eternal Thou: Ich und Du, p. 89; *I and Thou,* p. 75.

Realization vs. reflection: Ich und Du, p. 133; *I and Thou,* pp. 115 f.

God needs you: Ich und Du, p. 97; *I and Thou,* p. 82.

Thinking: See "A conversion." *Between Man and Man,* p. 28.

The third alternative: From *Baayat ha-adam,* Tel Aviv, 1943, based on lectures at the Hebrew University, Jerusalem, Summer, 1939; "Das Problem des Menschen," *Dialogisches Leben,* Zürich, 1947; "What Is Man?," *Between Man and Man,* pp. 204 f.

In our age: From "God and the Spirit of Man," *Eclipse of God,* pp. 166 f. Tr. Maurice Friedman.

Hope: From "Hope for this Hour," an address in New York at the conclusion of Buber's lecture tour in the United States in 1951. *Pointing the Way,* New York, 1957, pp. 228 f.

III. FAITH

Into my very life: See "A conversion." *Between Man and Man,* p. 12.

Meaning: See "Transcendence." *Eclipse of God,* pp. 49 f. Tr. Maurice Friedman.

Fear of God: See "Transcendence." *Eclipse of God,* pp. 50 f. Tr. Maurice Friedman.

The deed: See "Not what but how." *Reden über das Judentum,* pp. 122 f. *On Judaism,* pp. 93 f.

The ethical aspect: From "Religion and Ethics," *Eclipse of God,* pp. 128 f. Tr. Eugene Kamenka and Maurice Friedman.

Direction: See "Spinoza." *The Origin and Meaning of Hasidism,* pp. 98 f.

Prayer: From "God and the Spirit of Man," *Eclipse of God,*
p. 163. Tr. Maurice Friedman.

Biblical humanism: From *Der Morgen* IX-X (1933); *Ha-ruah
veha-metziut,* Tel Aviv, 1942, pp. 57 f.; "Hebrew Humanism,"
Israel and the World, pp. 246 f.

Religious humanism: From an address in Amsterdam, Holland,
upon accepting the Erasmus Prize, 1963. *Nachlese,* Heidelberg, 1965, pp. 114 and 118 f.

The danger of "religion": See "Spinoza." *The Origin and Meaning of Hasidism,* p. 94.

The existing God: From "God and the Spirit of Man," *Eclipse
of God,* p. 159. Tr. Maurice Friedman.

Reciprocity: See "Transcendence." *Eclipse of God,* p. 46.

Knowledge: See "Transcendence." *Eclipse of God,* p. 58.

Reading the Bible: From *Die Schrift und ihre Verdeutschung,*
Berlin, 1936, pp. 18 f.; the essay is based on a series of lectures
given in 1926. "The Man of Today and the Jewish Bible,"
Israel and the World, p. 93.

Spirituality: See "Images." *Israel and the World,* pp. 43 f.

To youth: From "Cheruth"; *Reden über das Judentum,*
pp. 204 f. *On Judaism,* p. 152.

One front: From an address at the University of Hamburg,
Germany, upon accepting the Goethe Prize, June, 1953.
Hinweise, Zürich, 1953, p. 345; "The Validity and Limitation
of the Political Principle," *Pointing the Way,* pp. 218 f.

Courage and love: From an address at the Lehrhaus in Frank-
furt/Main, Germany, October, 1934. *Die Stunde und die
Erkenntnis,* Frankfurt/Main, 1936, p. 78; "The Power of the
Spirit," *Israel and the World,* p. 176.

IV. MAN

Man—an audacity of life: From *Bilder von Gut und Böse,*
Cologne, 1952, pp. 102 f.; *Images of Good and Evil,* London,
1952, pp. 76 f.

The threefold relation: See "The third alternative." *Between
Man and Man,* p. 177.

Independence: From "Religion and Ethics," *Eclipse of God*, p. 138. Tr. Eugene Kamenka and Maurice Friedman.

We: From "What Is Common to All," *Review of Metaphysics* XI (1958); *The Knowledge of Man*, p. 108. Tr. Maurice Friedman.

Perfected relation: From "Man and His Image-Work," *Portfolio* VII (1963); *The Knowledge of Man*, pp. 163 f. Tr. Maurice Friedman.

Truth: See "Images." *Israel and the World*, p. 46.

One lives it: From "The Place of Hasidism in the History of Religion," *The Origin and Meaning of Hasidism*, p. 229.

Totality: See "Courage and love." *Israel and the World*, p. 175.

Circumstances: See "Thinking." *Between Man and Man*, p. 39.

Nothing but the image: See "Response." *Between Man and Man*, pp. 102 f.

Education: From a lecture at the Lehrhaus, Frankfurt/Main, Germany, January, 1935. *Die Stunde und die Erkenntnis*, pp. 126 f.; *Pointing the Way*, p. 105.

Contact: From a radio address in Jerusalem, 1950. *Nachlese*, pp. 93 f.

Socratic and Mosaic man: From an address at the Lehrhaus in Frankfurt/Main, April, 1934. *Die Stunde und die Erkenntnis*, p. 67; *Israel and the World*, p. 141.

The struggle: From *Die Frage an den Einzelnen*, Berlin, 1936, an elaboration of a lecture to university students in Switzerland, November, 1933. *Between Man and Man*, p. 70.

This beloved thing: From "Mit einem Monisten," written in 1914; *Ereignisse und Begegnungen*, Leipzig, 1920; *Hinweise*, Zürich, 1953, pp. 41 f.; *Pointing the Way*, pp. 28 f.

Human pursuits: See "This beloved thing." *Pointing the Way*, pp. 29 f.

Death: "Nach dem Tod," written in response to a questionnaire, 1927. *Nachlese*, p. 127.

Satan: From an address at Frankfurt/Main, Germany, September, 1953, accepting the Peace Prize of the German Book Trade. "Genuine Dialogue and the Possibilities of Peace," *Pointing the Way*, p. 239.

V. HUMAN SPEECH AND DIALOGUE

Language and address: From "The Word That Is Spoken," *Modern Age* V, 4 (Fall, 1961); *The Knowledge of Man,* pp. 115 f. Tr. Maurice Friedman.

Distance and relation: See "Language and address." *The Knowledge of Man,* pp. 117 f.

The partner: From "Elements of the Interhuman," *Psychiatry* XX, 2 (May, 1957); *The Knowledge of Man,* p. 85. Tr. Ronald Gregor Smith.

Without reserve: See "The partner." *The Knowledge of Man,* p. 86.

Three elements: See "Language and address." *The Knowledge of Man,* p. 120.

Sharing of knowledge: See "We." *The Knowledge of Man,* p. 106. Tr. Maurice Friedman.

The central question: See "Hope." *Pointing the Way,* p. 222.

The "narrow ridge": See "The third alternative." *Between Man and Man,* p. 184.

Unity of contraries: See "Ethics." *Israel and the World,* p. 17.

Acceptance of otherness: See "Limits." *The Knowledge of Man,* p. 69.

The sphere of "between": See "The third alternative." *Between Man and Man,* pp. 202 f.

Living with one another: See "We." *The Knowledge of Man,* p. 107.

The Christian and the Jew: See "A conversion." *Between Man and Man,* pp. 5 f.

Religious conversations: See "A conversion." *Between Man and Man,* pp. 7 f.

The signs: See "A conversion." *Between Man and Man,* pp. 10 f.

Love: See "A conversion." *Between Man and Man,* pp. 20 f.

The break-through: See "A conversion." *Between Man and Man,* pp. 35 f.

In this hour: See "Satan." *Pointing the Way,* p. 238.

The word: See "Satan." *Pointing the Way,* p. 236.

Crisis: See "Satan." *Pointing the Way,* p. 237.

Books and men: From "Bücher und Menschen," written in 1947; *Hinweise*, p. 9; *Pointing the Way*, p. 4.

Voices: See "A conversion." *Between Man and Man*, p. 15.

VI. CREATION—REVELATION—REDEMPTION

Hallowing: See "Courage and love." *Israel and the World*, pp. 180 f.

Purpose: From a public lecture in Tel Aviv, 1939. *Ha-ruah veha-Metziut*, p. 25. "The Spirit of Israel and the World of Today," *Israel and the World*, p. 186.

Grace: See "Spirit and nature." *Kampf um Israel*, p. 57; *Israel and the World*, pp. 32 f.

Fellow-creatures: From *Die Frage an den Einzelnen*, p. 34; "The Question to the Single One," *Between Man and Man*, p. 52.

The stamp of truth: See "Dualism." *Israel and the World*, p. 235.

Whence evil?: See "Spinoza." *The Origin and Meaning of Hasidism*, pp. 100 f.

With all of one's soul: From the address "Der Geist des Orients und das Judentum," *Vom Geist des Judentums*, Leipzig, 1916, pp. 26 f., *Reden über das Judentum*, p. 82. *On Judaism*, p. 66.

Meet the world: From an address in New York, November-December, 1951, as the Israel Goldstein Lecture for that year, under the auspices of the Jewish Theological Seminary. "The Silent Question," *At the Turning*, New York, 1952, p. 44. *On Judaism*, pp. 212 f.

The basis: See "Reading the Bible." *Die Schrift und ihre Verdeutschung*, p. 27; *Israel and the World*, p. 99.

From without: From an address, in 1928, on "Philosophische und religiöse Weltanschauung in der Erwachsenenbildung." *Tagungsbericht des Hohenrodter Bundes* II, Berlin, 1929. *Nachlese*, pp. 134 f.

Authentication: From *Bilder von Gut und Böse*, pp. 111 f.; *Images of Good and Evil*, p. 83.

Commandment: From "Goyim ve-elohav," *Keneset . . . le-ze-kher H. N. Bialik* VI (1941); "The Gods of the Nations and God," *Israel and the World,* p. 209.

God and the neighbor: See "Fellow-creatures." *Between Man and Man,* pp. 51 f.

Reason and revelation: From "Fragmente über Offenbarung," written at different times; *Nachlese,* pp. 107 f.

The touch of the other: See "The basis." *Israel and the World,* pp. 98 f.

Beginning and end: See "The basis." *Israel and the World,* pp. 95 f.

Body, soul, and spirit: See "Unity of contraries." *Israel and the World,* p. 27.

Between creation and redemption: See "Spinoza." *The Origin and Meaning of Hasidism,* pp. 105 f.

Messianic action: See "Spinoza." *The Origin and Meaning of Hasidism,* pp. 111 f.

The moment: From "Sinnbildliche und sakramentale Existenz im Judentum," based on a lecture at a convention on the history of religion in Ascona, Switzerland, 1934; *Deutung des Chassidismus,* Berlin, 1935, pp. 92 f.; "Symbolic and Sacramental Existence," *The Origin and Meaning of Hasidism,* p. 181.

Jews and Christians: See "Grace." *Israel and the World,* pp. 39 f.

All the spheres of man: See "The *polis* of God." *Pointing the Way,* p. 137.

God waits for man: See "Spinoza." *Pointing the Way,* p. 104.

VII. COMMUNITY AND HISTORY

Life in common: From *Netivot be-utopia,* Tel Aviv, 1947 (written in 1945); "In the Midst of Crisis," *Paths in Utopia,* New York, 1950, pp. 134 f.

Center: See "Life in common." *Paths in Utopia,* p. 135.

The polis of God: From "Gandhi, die Politik und wir," *Die Gandhi-Revolution,* ed. F. Diettrich, 1930; appendix to *Die Frage an den Einzelnen;* "Gandhi, Politics, and Us," *Pointing the Way,* p. 131.

Religious socialism: From "Drei Sätze eines religiösen Sozialismus," *Neue Wege* XXII (1928); *Hinweise,* pp. 259 f.; *Pointing the Way,* p. 112.

Religion and socialism: See "Religious socialism." *Pointing the Way,* pp. 113 f.

Socialism: See "Life in common." "Landauer," *Paths in Utopia,* p. 56.

Pseudo-realization: See "Life in common." "The Utopian Element in Socialism," *Paths in Utopia,* p. 15.

Three covenants: From the address in May, 1918, "Der heilige Weg," Frankfurt/Main, 1919; *Reden über das Judentum,* pp. 150 f. *On Judaism,* pp. 112 f.

State: See "Life in common." "Lenin," *Paths in Utopia,* p. 104.

Meaning of history: From "Geschehende Geschichte," written Summer, 1933; *Die Stunde und die Erkenntnis,* pp. 32 f.; "In the Midst of History," *Israel and the World,* pp. 81 f.

Goals: See "Dualism." *Israel and the World,* pp. 238 f.

Freedom: See "Nothing but the image." *Between Man and Man,* p. 91.

The revolutionary: From "Erinnerung an einen Tod" [on Gustav Landauer], *Neue Wege* XXIII, 4 (1929); *Hinweise,* p. 256; *Pointing the Way,* p. 118.

Power: From an address at the Twelfth Zionist Congress, at Karlsbad, September 5, 1921. *Kampf um Israel,* p. 228; *Israel and the World,* p. 216.

Will to power: From "Am u-manhig," *Moznayim* XIV, 3 (1942); "People and Leader," *Pointing the Way,* pp. 157 f.

Religion and politics: See "The polis of God." *Pointing the Way,* p. 128.

Non-action: From an address at a conference of the China Institut, Frankfurt/Main, Germany, Fall, 1928; *Chinesisch-deutscher Almanach für das Jahr Gi Si 1929-30,* Frankfurt/Main, 1929. *Nachlese,* pp. 210 ff.; *Pointing the Way,* pp. 124 f.

Transformation: From "Prophetie, Apokalyptik und die geschichtliche Stunde," *Merkur* VIII, 12 (1954); *Sehertum,* Cologne, 1955, p. 74; "Prophecy, Apocalyptic, and the Historical Hour," *Pointing the Way,* pp. 206 f.

History and eternity: See "One front." *Pointing the Way,* p. 215.

War and peace: See "Satan." *Pointing the Way*, pp. 234 f.

The covenant of men: See "The *polis* of God." *Pointing the Way*, pp. 137 f.

VIII. ISRAEL: JEWISH EXISTENCE

Life itself: See "Spinoza." *The Origin and Meaning of Hasidism*, pp. 91 f.

Unity: From the address "Das Judentum und die Menschheit," *Reden über das Judentum*, p. 27; one of the original "Three addresses," published in 1911. *On Judaism*, p. 28.

Teaching and life: See "Socratic and Mosaic man." *Israel and the World*, p. 140.

Presence: See "Three covenants." *Reden über das Judentum*, p. 146.

In heaven and on earth: See "Grace." *Israel and the World*, pp. 30 f.

Memory: From a syllabus for the School for Jewish Youth in Berlin, 1932. *Kampf um Israel*, p. 136; *Israel and the World*, p. 146. *On Judaism*, p. 109.

The God of Sinai: See "Dualism." *Israel and the World*, pp. 236 f.

The King: From an address "Politik aus dem Glauben," May 1, 1933. *Nachlese*, pp. 190 f.

Prophetic criticism: From the inaugural lecture at the Hebrew University, Jerusalem, 1938. *Ha-ruah veha-metziut*, p. 17; "The Demand of the Spirit and Historical Reality," *Pointing the Way*, pp. 188 f.

The Ten Commandments: From a response to a questionnaire; *Literarische Welt*, June 7, 1929. "What Are We to Do About the Ten Commandments?" *Israel and the World*, p. 85.

Covenant: From "Humaniut ivrit," *Hapoel Hatzair* XXXIV, 18 (May 30, 1941); *Ha-ruah veha-metziut*, p. 59; *Israel and the World*, pp. 248 f.

Biblical leadership: From a lecture in Munich, Germany, 1928; "Biblisches Führertum," *Kampf um Israel*, pp. 102 f; *Israel and the World*, pp. 131 f.

Success and failure: See "Biblical leadership." *Israel and the World,* p. 125.

Prophetic faith: See "Transformation." *Pointing the Way,* pp. 197 f.

Prophecy and apocalyptic: See "Transformation." *Pointing the Way,* p. 203.

Community: From an address at the Lehrhaus in Frankfurt/ Main, January, 1943; *Die Stunde und die Erkenntnis,* pp. 45 f.; "The Jew in the World," *Israel and the World,* p. 170.

The message of Hasidism: From "Hasidism and Modern Man," *Between East and West:* Essays dedicated to the memory of Bela Horovitz, ed. A. Altmann, London, 1958, pp. 20 f.

To Gandhi: From "A Letter to Gandhi," February 24, 1939. Martin Buber and Judah Magnes, *Two Letters to Gandhi,* Jerusalem, 1939; *Pointing the Way,* p. 146.

On accepting a German award: See "Satan." *Pointing the Way,* pp. 233 f.

Peace: From an address at a convention of Jewish youth representatives in Antwerp, Belgium, July, 1932; "Wann denn?" *Kampf um Israel,* pp. 459 f.; "And If Not Now, When?" *Israel and the World,* p. 239.

Another world?: See "The king." *Nachlese,* pp. 190 f.

The kingdom of God: See "Community." *Israel and the World,* p. 171.

EPILOGUE: RENEWAL

Renewal of relation: See "Hope." *Pointing the Way,* pp. 224 f.

The neighbor: From a draft for a preface to E. A. Gutkind, *Community and Environment; Nachlese,* pp. 84 f.

Confirmation: See "Limits." *The Knowledge of Man,* p. 71.

Thanksgiving: "Danksagung," in response to letters received by Buber on the occasion of his eightieth birthday in 1958. *Du sollst ein Segen sein,* Graz, 1964; *Nachlese,* p. 254.